4/80

The Art of Making
CLOTH TOYS

The Art of Making
CLOTH TOYS

CHARLENE DAVIS ROTH

CHILTON BOOK COMPANY RADNOR, PENNSYLVANIA

Copyright © 1974 by Charlene Davis Roth
All Rights Reserved
Published in Radnor, Pa., by Chilton
Book Company and simultaneously in Ontario,
Canada, by Thomas Nelson & Sons, Ltd.
Designed by William E. Lickfield
Photographs by James A. Davis
Manufactured in the United States of America

Library of Congress Cataloging in Publication Data

Roth, Charlene Davis, 1945-
    The art of making cloth toys.
    1. Soft toy making. I. Title.
TT174.3.R67 1974   745.59'24   74-865
ISBN 0-8019-5870-9
ISBN 0-8019-5871-7 (pbk.)

2 3 4 5 6 7 8 9   6 5 4 3 2 1 0 9

To MICHAEL B. ALTMAN

Contents

List of Illustrations

vii

Color Illustrations

Introduction

History

Although the doll was in existence during prehistoric times, the toy doll is a product of civilization. In ancient times, the doll served as idol, ancestor image, fetish, talisman, votive image—forms in which inanimate materials became invested with occult and religious significance.

It took thousands of years for dolls to evolve into playthings, first surfacing in this light among the artifacts of early civilizations. The ancient Egyptians, for example, had toy dolls made of wood or linen, stuffed with papyrus strips. The Greeks made toy dolls of clay and occasionally of plaster or wax. During the Middle Ages, dolls were made of cloth, clay, and wood and were often stuffed with rags or sawdust.

It wasn't until the nineteenth century that technology helped produce a more durable and sophisticated doll. New materials were used, such as china, bisque, papier mâché, and rubber. Mirroring the advances in mechanics, dolls became more complicated. The ball joint was used to make limbs flexible and necks movable. Eyes opened and shut. In the 1820s, dolls that walked and talked were introduced.

Today, in the twentieth century, plastics and electronics have revolutionized the world of the doll. They are more lifelike and complex than ever. With the push of a button or the pull of a string, dolls walk, talk, sing, dance, smile, cry, wet their diapers.

Having a variety of precocious and dexterous toy dolls on display at your neighborhood toystore, you might wonder why anyone should bother to make a doll of cloth, for it won't be as anatomically detailed or as mechanically versatile.

As you probably have guessed, I have a number of reasons that favor handcrafted cloth dolls over factory produced androids. First, there are simple economic reasons. A homemade doll costs less. You can use odds and ends, old clothing, and scraps of fabric. Even if you have to buy all the materials, it shouldn't cost more than $2 or $3 to make an elaborate cloth doll from scratch.

Then there's the feeling of accomplishment and enjoyment you get from making something yourself. Designing and assembling your own toys, your own dresses, or your own model airplanes is a most satisfying experience.

Handmade toys are unique and individual. No two handsewn dolls are the same. I have made several cloth toys from the same pattern and they always turn out different. Because they are not mass produced, not as interchangeable as standard mechanical parts, you can bet that the youngster up the road or down the block won't have an identical replica, even if he or she has a doll made from the same set of instructions.

Making a toy for a child is a much more intimate experience than buying one, a direct transference of your affection into a tangible shape and form. Children can become partners in the creation of their own toys. They can pick out the fabrics and the colors they like. If they are old enough, they can help with the simpler aspects of assembly.

Toys are receptacles for a child's imagination, containers for their fantasies, companions for their joys and sorrows. Isn't it better to let your own subtle feelings shape your children's playthings than to trust a distant, faceless designer employed by a mass producing toy manufacturer motivated by profit and loss, supply and demand?

Using Your Creativity

Often, when writing a craft book, the tendency is to be more explicit than is necessary in the hope that the reader will be successful and turn out an exact replica of what the author has in mind. This attitude tends to be dictatorial and the crafts produced are not as individual as you expect of handmade things. In this book, I have tried to fight that tendency and leave loopholes for your imagination to fill. The techniques and instructions for making the dolls are explained in detail, but there are areas which have been left without strict guidelines.

One area I've left open-ended is the choice of fabrics. At the beginning of each project, I've given the yardages (of material 36 inches wide) necessary to complete the toy, but have only suggested the type and design of fabrics you might use. Keep in mind that certain properties are desirable when making a cloth toy, such as durability, washability, and texture. Aside from that, let your imagination roam free. Don't be afraid to experiment with unusual colors or to mix prints. If you prefer bright colors, use bright fabric. If you want subtle colors, choose the fabric accordingly. If you think a particular doll should be smooth rather than furry, or silky instead of rough, make it that way.

Oftentimes when searching through the remnant counters of your local fabric stores, a piece of fabric will suggest a toy to you. You don't have to pick the doll first and then look for the fabric. A bright brown and orange print could bring to mind a camel; a fluffy piece of imitation fur might suggest a teddy bear. Or you might find striped black and white cotton just perfect for a zebra, a toy not discussed in this book—but don't despair. Chapter 1 contains information about designing your own toys or redesigning some that are included here. One or two changes and Horatio Horse becomes Zelda Zebra!

Trimming is another area for improvisation. Your notions counters are overflowing with lace, sequins, ribbons and buttons. Decorate the dolls with abandon. Stitch rows of sequins to the dresses and gowns, trim panties and hats with lace, use fringe and decorative tape to spruce up a jacket or a shirt. Make braid harnesses for the animals. If you can embroider, there's no end to the possibilities for trimming the toys. Embroider everything from hair to flowers to features. Add your own touches to the features also. In most cases, a slight alteration gives a very different look. Use almond-shaped eyes instead of circles; add eyelashes or eyebrows where there are none; change a smile to a frown, or add a tongue or teeth or both.

From the instructions in this book, you can learn the basics for making cloth toys, but don't feel bound by them. Feel free to make changes and experiment with your own ideas.

Chapter 1

Procedures and Techniques

THE procedures for assembling the cloth toys in this book generally follow the same order, from the simplest to the most complex. First the patterns are enlarged, cut from paper, and pinned to the fabric chosen for the toy. Then the fabric is cut into pieces to match the patterns. Markings are transferred to the fabric cutouts. If the toy requires a lining, it is lined here. Next the fabric cutouts are sewn together to form a cloth shell and the shell is stuffed. Finally, clothing, if any, is constructed and the features and other decorations are added.

Before you begin to work on any toy, I would suggest that you first read through the entire chapter and examine all the relevant drawings, patterns, and photographs. Procedural instructions that seem confusing in the reading will become clear as you complete the actual steps of assembly.

The simpler toys are at the beginning of the book, the more complex at the end. Early chapters teach techniques and skills that prepare you for the more difficult toys.

CHOOSING FABRICS

The toys in this book require only small amounts of fabrics, a yard at the most. You can search the remnant tables at your local fabric store or rummage through your closet for clothing you no longer intend to wear. When choosing fabrics for toys, there are special qualities you should look for: durability, washability, texture, color, and design.

Durability and strength are the most important features for consideration. A cloth toy is subjected to a great deal of wear and tear: it is chewed

1

on, dragged around, slept upon, and hugged. Use medium-weight or heavyweight fabrics to ensure a long life for the toy. Examples are cotton duck, sail cloth, cotton corduroy, and denim. There are a variety of other fabrics sufficiently sturdy. Trust your fingers to feel the fabrics and be sure they are durable enough. Although knits and stretch fabrics are very popular (they come in enticing colors and bright prints), I don't recommend their use for the bodies of cloth toys. Stretch fabrics are extremely difficult to stuff. They won't hold the shape they are meant to represent. However, you can use them to make clothing for the dolls.

Try to use fabrics that are washable and colorfast; a child will give a favorite cloth toy the same rough treatment as a pair of dungarees. When you buy fabric, check the labels or ask the clerk about the properties of the fabric. If you use old clothing, check the labels.

The texture of fabrics is important, as is color and design. Texture gives a toy personality and makes it more realistic. Fur fabrics, for example, are ideal for animals. Fabric textures vary from smooth, shiny satins to soft napped, brushed denim to long, shaggy fake fur. Color and design should be considered too. Try to choose colors and designs that suit the character of the toy you are making. Below are some useful fabrics and their properties.

Cottons: Medium and heavyweight cottons are strong and washable and come in a spectrum of colors, prints, and plaids. Check to be sure the fabric has been treated for shrinkage and colorfastness. Some cotton fabrics I particularly like are: no-wale corduroy, because it has a nap and comes in rich colors; sail cloth and cotton duck, because they are strong and come in bright prints; brushed denim, because of its nap, durability, and colors; and cotton flannel, because it is an ideal lining fabric.

Felt: Felt is made from wool fibers that have been pressed together. Felt has no raw edges and is therefore ideal for features and appliqués. Choose a good quality as the lighter weight felts pull apart easily.

Taffeta or Satin: Both are smooth, crisp shiny fabrics and come in a variety of bright iridescent colors. They make an attractive contrast when used in combination with other fabrics for the bellies and inner ears of the animal dolls.

ENLARGING THE PATTERNS

Some patterns, such as features, are represented here in actual size. Most others, because their actual size is larger than the pages of this book, have been reduced and you will have to enlarge them. This is very easy to do.

You need a piece of paper, like newsprint or wrapping paper, large enough to accommodate the overall dimensions of the design. You need a ruler, a marker to draw the lines of the graph, and a pencil with an eraser so that you can make changes as you draw the patterns.

First count the number of squares horizontally and vertically on the graph of the pattern you want to enlarge. Then draw the enlarged graph on paper, with each square measuring 2 × 2 inches. You will then have a graph with the same number of squares as the graph in the book, but much larger (Fig. 1-1).

Next transfer the patterns from the book to the enlarged graph. Work carefully, square by square. In this manner, you will be able to produce an enlargement as accurate as the original. Be sure to transfer all dots, dashes, dotted lines, notches, numbers, and letters to the enlarged patterns. After the patterns are enlarged, they are cut from the paper, then pinned to the fabric.

NOTE: All of the patterns in this book that have to be enlarged will come out the intended size if you use a graph on which each square measures 2 × 2 inches.

1-1   Enlarging a pattern

CUTTING

Press all fabrics before you cut them. Each pattern has a number on it that indicates the number of pieces to be cut (cut 1, cut 2, etc.). Make sure you cut the correct number of pieces. Single pattern pieces are cut from a single thickness of fabric. In those instances where two pieces are required from the same pattern, you can use a double thickness of fabric and cut both pieces at the same time. When a pattern is marked "place this edge along fold of fabric when cutting," it means you fold your fabric to a double thickness and pin the pattern piece to the fabric with the marked edge parallel to the fold. Cut around the outline of the pattern, but not along the fold. When the pattern is unpinned, you will have cut a single piece of fabric twice the size of the pattern. Don't unpin the patterns from the fabric until you transfer the markings.

TRANSFERRING MARKINGS

The markings on the pattern (dots, lines, numbers, etc.) have to be transferred to the fabric. These markings are aids to help you assemble the toys and to place features and decorations. Dressmaker's tracing paper is ideal for transferring these markings. You can buy it anywhere notions or sewing accessories are sold.

To transfer the markings, first choose a color of dressmaker's tracing paper that will show up on the fabric you are using: white tracing paper for dark fabrics, navy blue tracing paper for light fabrics. The tracing paper is sandwiched between the fabric and the pattern, with the colored side of the tracing paper against the side of the fabric you intend to mark. Pin the pattern, tracing paper, and fabric together so they won't slip. Now the markings on the pattern are traced over with a pointed instrument, like a knitting needle or a blunt pencil. Use only enough pressure to get a visible line on the fabric. Too much pressure will tear the pattern (Fig. 1-2). After you finish tracing the markings, remove the pins and check for accuracy.

LINING

Most of the toys in this book are lined. Lining strengthens surface fabrics and helps to prevent the loss of stuffing if a toy is torn. The same patterns used to cut the basic parts of the toys are used for the lining and the same number of pieces are cut. For example, if you are instructed to cut two body pieces, you also cut two lining pieces, one for each body piece. Lining is always pinned and sewn to the wrong side (the side that doesn't show when the assembly is completed) of the fabric. You don't transfer markings to the lining. Features, appliqés, soles of the feet, and decorations don't have to be lined.

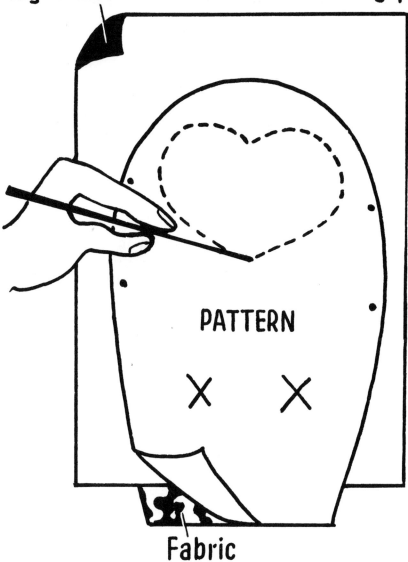

Right side of dressmaker's tracing paper

PATTERN

X X

Fabric

1-2   Transferring markings

SEWING

You can sew the toys entirely by hand; however, unless you're unalterably opposed to mechanical devices, I recommend the major part of the sewing be done by machine. Check your sewing machine manual to find the proper tension and pressure settings for the particular fabric you are working on. I prefer a setting of 12 to 15 stitches to the inch, as it assures a tight seam. Unless otherwise stated, ¼ inch of fabric is allowed for seams, meaning your stitches are ¼ inch within the outer edge of the fabric. Where special hand stitches or machine settings are required, the instructions and explanations are given in the text.

STUFFING

Because the stuffing pretty much determines the final appearance of the toy, it is important to master the techniques. Mainly it takes patience. The trick is to stuff the toy slowly and to use small wads of stuffing, approximately the size of a plum. Larger chunks of stuffing tend to make a lumpy toy with a wrinkled surface. Get yourself a good stuffing tool. I suggest a large aluminum crochet hook, the eraser end of a pencil, or a ½-inch wooden dowel.

I recommend two kinds of stuffing material, kapok or Dacron® (also called polyester fiber). Kapok is easy to work with and is less expensive than Dacron, but it has several drawbacks. It isn't washable; some people are allergic to it; and unless you live in a large city, you'll have trouble finding a store that sells it. Dacron costs more, but it is washable, only slightly more difficult to work with, and is readily available at most chain discount stores.

There are many other materials you can use for stuffing a cloth toy. Shredded foam rubber, scraps or strips of fabric, straw, even newspaper. You can also salvage stuffing material from old upholstery, pillows, or other stuffed toys too old or worn to repair.

Toys are stuffed either lightly, moderately, or firmly:

> *Lightly stuffed:* loose pads of stuffing, sufficient to barely fill out the shape.
> *Moderately stuffed:* dense enough to thoroughly fill out the curves and cavities, but loose enough for the toy to remain squeezably soft and bendable.
> *Firmly stuffed:* wads of stuffing packed tight enough so that the surface of the doll is smooth to the touch and resilient, but not so firm that seams are strained.

DECORATING THE SURFACE

Features and decorative touches are either glued and sewn to the fabric, painted on, or appliquéd. There are special cloth glues you can buy that are of good quality, inexpensive, and easy to locate. I prefer liquid latex. It is an ideal adhesive for gluing cloth. You can purchase it at most hobby, craft, or art supply stores. After you glue a piece, let it dry before you stitch it to the surface fabric. Liquid latex dries in 15 minutes.

Clear nylon thread is perfect for surface stitching. It is very strong and almost invisible. To make nylon thread easier to handle, cut a length of it and then run it against a chunk of wax. For sewing features and appliqués, I prefer very slender, sharp needles because they tend to curve slightly, which makes it easier to sew a taut surface.

For those toys that require painted features, use a good brand of non-toxic acrylic paint and apply the paint with a small sable brush. Acrylic paint is water soluble when wet, but dries to an insoluble plastic. Coating the fabric with acrylic gesso before you paint the features prevents the paint from being absorbed into the stuffing, and thereby losing definition and clarity. Afterwards, coat the painted areas with gloss or mat acrylic varnish.

NECESSARY AND HELPFUL TOOLS

Bodkin or Large Safety Pin: A bodkin is an instrument with a safety pin closing at one end. It is used to draw elastic through a casing. Though not quite so handy, a large safety pin serves the same purpose.

Crochet Hooks: Crochet hooks in various sizes are used for crocheting chains to decorate the toys. A large aluminum crochet hook also makes an excellent stuffing tool.

Iron and Ironing Board: These are indispensable. Pressing is required in various stages of assembly and it is advisable to press all fabrics before cutting. Although a steam iron is useful, you can obtain the same results by placing a damp cloth between your iron and the fabric.

Needles: An all purpose pack of household needles is a good investment. These assortments usually contain a curved mattress needle, a sharp needle with a large eye for sewing yarn, and a variety of other needles of many kinds and sizes. You will also find use for embroidery needles and knitting needles.

Pins and Pincushion: Get pins that have colored beads at the end. They are ideal for toymaking because they are easily visible. You want to be sure to remove each and every pin before you turn a toy right side out. A pincushion is an efficient and safe device for keeping pins in one place.

Pliers: A small pair comes in handy for making armatures.

Scissors: This is one of the most important pieces of equipment. I recommend that you have three pairs: a 7-inch pair of dressmaking shears for cutting the patterns from the fabric; a 5-inch pair of scissors for most of the utility work; and a 3½-inch pair to cut out features and other fine work.

Sewing Machine: Any machine will do as long as it stitches a tight seam.

Seam Ripper: An implement to make ripping out seams easier.

Stuffing Tool: A blunt instrument, like the eraser end of a pencil or a dowel, to push wads of stuffing into the cavities of the toys.

Tape Measure: A utility tool that is used for many jobs.

Tweezers: An indispensable tool for turning assembled pieces right side out.

Wax: A chunk of beeswax helps to make clear nylon thread easier to handle.

Wire Cutters: A lightweight pair to cut armature wire.

ALTERING AND DESIGNING PATTERNS

The subject of designing patterns for cloth toys could fill an entire book, but I will give you a brief idea of what is involved in case you want to make changes on any of the patterns in this book or want to design some simple toys of your own.

Altering a pattern is very easy. Use the existing pattern, trace it onto a large sheet of paper. Then erase that part of the pattern you want to change and draw in your own modifications. You can move arms and legs, change the shape of the body or head, lengthen or shorten a neck, and so on. The entire toy can be made bigger or smaller by changing the ratio of the graph and making the other measurements in proportion.

To design your own stuffed doll, start with a single basic pattern and cut two identical pieces from it, then sew them together. Sister Pat and Brother Philly were designed this way (see Chap. 4). For this kind of toy, keep the shape as simple as possible. The closer you stay to basic shapes, such as the circle, square, rectangle, triangle, the better it will look when stuffed.

To design the pattern, draw a direct front view or a profile. Make your drawing slightly larger than the finished toy, allowing for ¼-inch seams around all edges. Spend some time with an eraser and keep simplifying the design. When you are satisfied, cut it out for your pattern, and proceed as you would for the toys in the book: pin, cut, sew, stuff, decorate. At first use scraps of fabric, for it takes a little experimentation to refine a design.

The more complicated toys generally have a basic profile pattern (like the simple toys described above), plus one or more gusset patterns. The gusset makes a toy more three-dimensional and lets you design more complicated shapes. To design the patterns for these kinds of toys, start with the profile, again allowing for ¼-inch seams. Although the design doesn't have to be as geometrical as for a two piece doll, I still recommend that you avoid sharp curves and intricate details. To make the gusset pattern, use a tape measure to find the distance, along the profile pieces, that the gusset will transverse. Remember, this is not a straight line measurement, but a measurement over and around any curves or humps in the profile. Next draw a rectangle with the overall length you have measured and a width between 1 and 2 inches, depending on the shape of your design.

Again, using your judgment, tailor the shape of the gusset at one or both ends so it will join the two profile pieces. Now cut out the pattern and proceed in the usual way.

Doll clothing is easy to design. You have to do a lot of measuring to ascertain lengths of sleeves and trousers, widths of torsos, neck sizes, and so on; but once you know the measurements, it's merely a matter of joining lines together. You can use one of the basic patterns in the book to start (Fig. 17-2) and make it longer for a gown, shorter for a shirt. If you hand sew your own clothing, you can easily incorporate the same principles and adapt any pattern; with the advantage, of course, of not having to make the doll's clothes as complicated: set-in sleeves and darts don't have to be included.

Keep in mind when you begin to design your own toys that children are not nearly as particular as you are. Your first attempt may seem like an utter failure to you, but some child will love it as much as if a master craftsman made it. So don't be discouraged. Each toy you make will be better than the last.

Chapter 2

The Owl and the Pussy-cat

The Owl and the Pussy-cat went to sea
  In a beautiful pea-green boat;
They took some honey, and plenty of money,
  Wrapped in a five-pound note.

The Owl and the Pussy-cat
Edward Lear

$\mathcal{S}$AILING along in their pea-green boat, the Owl and the Pussy-cat are an excellent pair to begin this venture into cloth toymaking. They are fairly easy to make; yet during their construction, you will encounter, in simplified versions, most of the techniques necessary for making the more complicated toys that follow.

The inspiration for the Owl and the Pussy-cat dolls comes, of course, from the poem by Edward Lear. He was a hunch-backed, epileptic man who wrote some of the most fantastic children's poetry, with the strangest array of characters, including a cigar-smoking duck who wears worsted socks. You may want to read some of his tales; and when you've gained a little skill from this book, make counterparts of your own.

When our cloth cat is finished, it will measure 8 inches in height. The owl will be 10 inches. Use a crisp, printed cotton fabric for both doll bodies. Their features, their arms, and the anchor appliqué on the boat are felt. The boat itself is corduroy. This set of dolls can be made entirely from scraps of fabric: four different prints can be used to cut the front and the back of both dolls. Following is the list of materials, with approximate yardages of fabric, and other dimensions needed to make the Owl, the Pussy-cat, and their boat.

2-1   Owl and Pussy-cat

MATERIALS

½ yard of medium-weight print cotton fabric for the two doll bodies.

½ yard of white cotton flannel to line the doll bodies.

A 9 × 12-inch piece of felt for the arms of the cat and the wings of the owl.

Scraps of felt, preferably black, white, pink, yellow brown, orange, green, for the features, inner ears, the anchors, and rope appliqués.

Four black-rimmed rhinestone buttons, with ½-inch diameters, for the eyes.

½ yard of pea-green, medium-weight cotton fabric for the boat.

Thread to match the fabric and clear nylon thread.

Kapok or Dacron for stuffing.

STEP ONE

Enlarge the patterns for the Owl, the Pussy-cat, and the boat (Fig. 2-2). Cut the pieces for the dolls, their features, the boat, and the anchor appliqués from the fabrics you have chosen. Be sure to cut the right number of pieces, as marked on the pattern. For instance, in this case, you must cut *four* wing pieces and *two* body pieces for the owl.

Next, transfer the markings from the owl pattern to the *right* side of *one* body piece. Transfer the markings to the owl's face mask. Transfer the markings from the cat pattern to the *right* side of *one* body piece. Transfer the markings for the anchor appliqué to the *right* side of *one* boat piece.

Now cut lining pieces only for the doll bodies. Pin the lining pieces to the wrong side of the corresponding pieces cut previously. It is not necessary to transfer markings to the lining fabric.

STEP TWO

Note: ¼-inch seams are allowed. Unless otherwise stated, stitch fabric with *right* sides together. Remove all pins before turning assembled pieces right side out.

Begin with the owl. Use a nontoxic cloth glue or liquid latex and glue the owl's face mask to the marked body piece, positioning the mask over the dotted lines that are marked in the same shape on the fabric. Glue one pupil to the center of each eye. Glue the beak to the face mask over the markings. Glue the eyes to the face mask, overlapping the beak. Glue the thighs to the same body piece, placing each over the large X's marked on the fabric. Glue the feet to the fabric, overlapping the lower edge of the thighs. Allow the

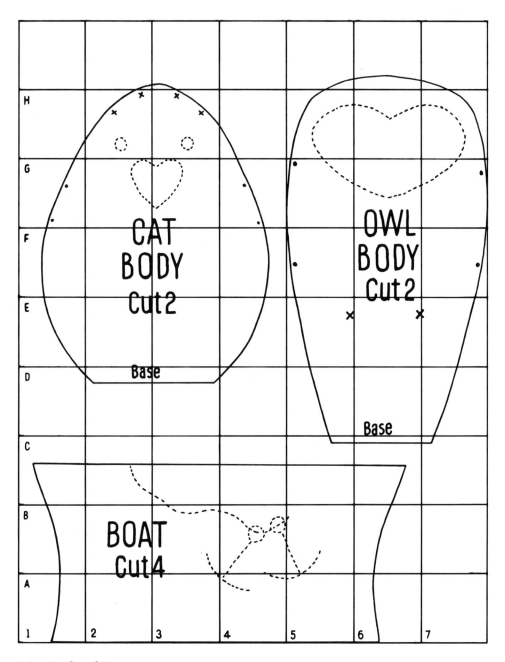

2-2 Owl and Pussy-cat

13

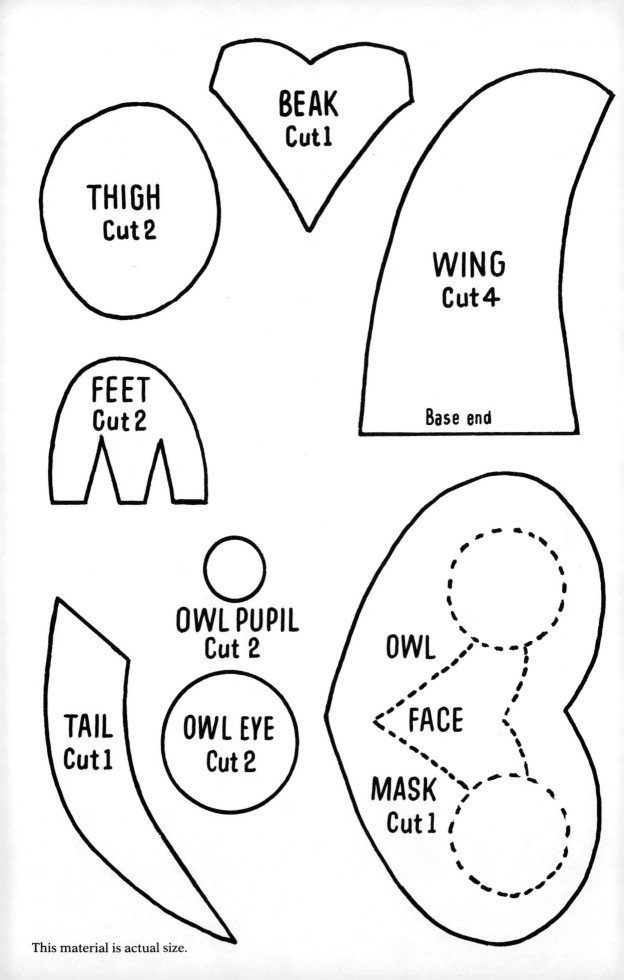

BEAK
Cut 1

THIGH
Cut 2

WING
Cut 4

Base end

FEET
Cut 2

OWL PUPIL
Cut 2

OWL

FACE

MASK
Cut 1

TAIL
Cut 1

OWL EYE
Cut 2

This material is actual size.

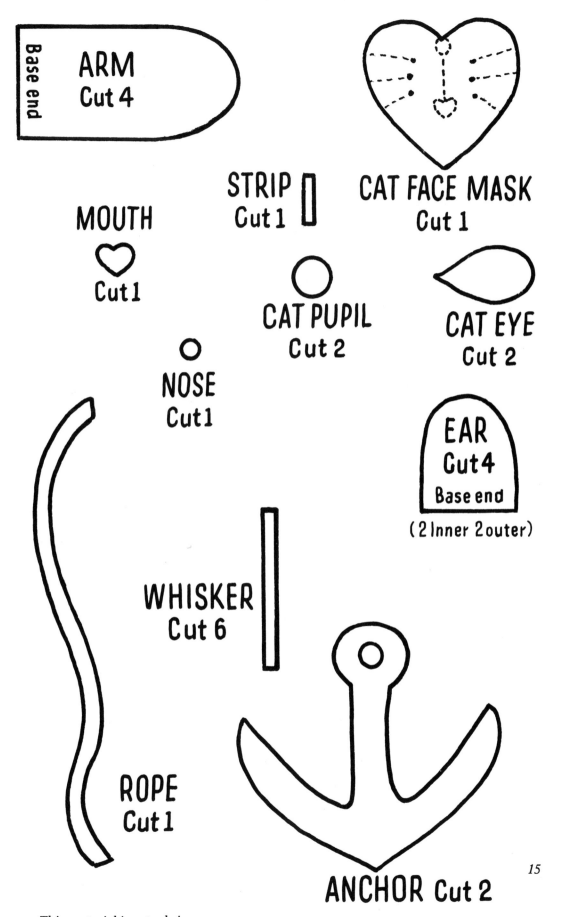

ARM
Cut 4

Base end

STRIP
Cut 1

CAT FACE MASK
Cut 1

MOUTH
Cut 1

CAT PUPIL
Cut 2

CAT EYE
Cut 2

NOSE
Cut 1

EAR
Cut 4
Base end
(2 Inner 2 outer)

WHISKER
Cut 6

ROPE
Cut 1

ANCHOR Cut 2

15

This material is actual size.

glue sufficient time to dry thoroughly. Then stitch the pieces to the fabric, using the appliqué stitch on your sewing machine or by stitching them down by hand with clear nylon thread.

The owl's wings are cut from felt. Because felt does not unravel, it may be topstitched together, which eliminates the necessity of turning the pieces right side out and helps provide a sharp line: difficult to achieve when the fabric has to be turned out. The next step here is to topstitch each pair of wing pieces together. Place a line of machine stitching ¼ inch inside the outer edge of the fabric. Leave the base end of the wings open. Gently pad each wing with stuffing.

Pin one wing to the *right* side of the *front* body piece, between the two dots marked on the fabric. The tip of the wing should curve up toward the face mask and the base end of the wing should extend ½ inch beyond the seamline (Fig. 2-3a). Pin the second wing to the owl's body between the second set of dots marked on the fabric. Baste both wings to the fabric. With *right* sides together, place the remaining piece of the owl's body over the body piece to which the wings are pinned. Baste the body pieces together by hand. This is to prevent slippage when stitching on the machine. Now stitch the two body pieces together, catching in the wings and leaving the *base* of the owl *open*. Turn the owl right side out and press.

The procedure for assembling the cat is practically the same as for the owl. First glue the cat's face mask over the dotted lines marked on the front body piece. Next glue the pupils to the eyes; then glue the eyes to the fabric just above the face mask, covering the circles marked on the fabric with dotted lines. Observe the markings on the face mask; glue to it the mouth, nose, strip, and whiskers. Now glue the cat's tail to the *right* side of the unmarked body piece, in the center of the lower back. After the glue has thoroughly dried, machine or hand stitch all these pieces to the fabric.

Topstitch the cat's arms together, placing the row of stitching ¼ inch inside the outer edge of the felt. Pad the arms lightly with stuffing. Pin the arms to the fabric, just as you did for the owl's wings (Fig. 2-3b). Baste the arms to the fabric.

With the *right* sides of the fabric together, stitch a pink inner ear to a pink outer ear, leaving the base of the ear open. Turn the ear right side out and topstitch close to the outer edge. Repeat for the second ear. With the pink sides down, pin the ears to the *right* side of the body front, fitting each ear between a pair of X's marked on the fabric (Fig. 2-3b). Baste the ears to the fabric.

With *right* sides together, place the back body piece over the body piece to which the arms and ears are pinned. Baste these body pieces together, then stitch around the entire perimeter, catching the arms and ears along the seamline, but leaving the base end open. Turn the cat right side out and press.

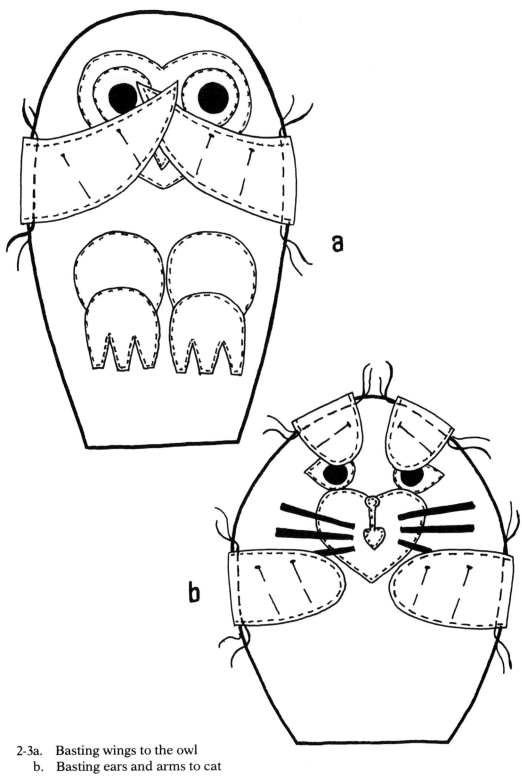

2-3a.　Basting wings to the owl
　　b.　Basting ears and arms to cat

Now begin the boat for the Owl and the Pussy-cat. Glue the anchors and the rope appliqués over the dotted lines on the *marked* boat piece. When the glue is dry, sew the appliqués to the fabric, by machine or by hand.

To assemble the boat, stitch two of the four boat pieces together around the entire perimeter, leaving a 2-inch opening in one side. Turn the piece right side out through the opening and press. Stitch the remaining two pieces together. Turn and press.

STEP THREE

It is of particular importance to master the techniques of stuffing simple shapes, such as the Owl and the Pussy-cat and the boat, so that you can progress to the more complex shapes without trouble. The stuffing should not be lumpy, but smooth and of uniform firmness. Any gaps or empty pockets will result in folds or creases, altering the surface appearance of the toy. Use small amounts of stuffing. Start with the upper half of the owl, carefully padding the stuffing along the seamline so that you end up with a neat and unrumpled curve. Stuff the remainder of the doll until it is full, but still soft. Turn ¼ inch of fabric around the edges of the base opening to the inside. Securely stitch the opening shut with clear nylon thread.

Repeat the above procedure and stuff the cat, then stitch shut the base opening.

The boat requires very little stuffing. Place only a layer approximately ⅛ inch thick inside each of the boat pieces. Turn ¼ inch of fabric around the opening edges of each piece to the inside. Stitch the openings shut.

STEP FOUR

Now for a few simple finishing touches. First sew a rhinestone button securely to the pupil of each eye of the Owl and the Pussy-cat.

Next, to complete the boat, topstitch along the upper edge of each boat piece, placing the line of stitching ¼ inch from the outer edge of the fabric. Topstitch the two boat pieces together at the sides and the base (Fig. 2-4). Again, place the line of stitching ¼ inch within the outer edge.

Place the Owl and the Pussy-cat side by side in their boat. They are now ready to sail away.

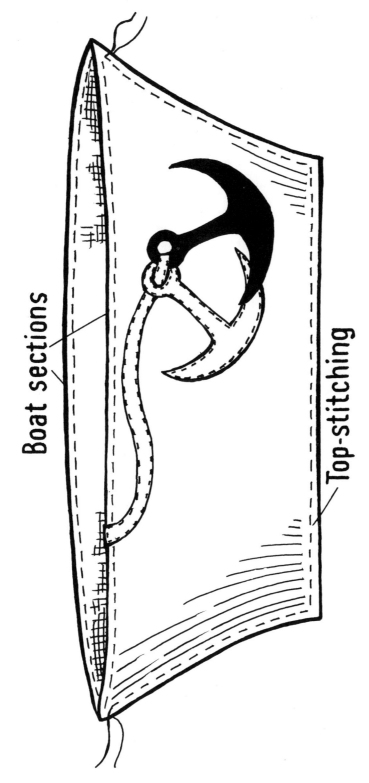

Boat sections

Top-stitching

2-4 Topstitching together the two sections of the boat

19

Chapter 3

Tallulah Ballerina

> With what eagerness she danced! Leaning on
> her partner's shoulder, twirling and whirling,
> her eyes sparkling, her cheeks flushed with ex-
> citement; and it was plain that she loved danc-
> ing better than anything else in the world.
>
> *The Twelve Dancing Princesses*
> Traditional German Fairytale

I GUESS that most young girls at one time or an-
other wish they could be ballerinas, for an enchanting aura surrounds the
dancer. She seems to twirl endlessly on the tips of her satin clad toes, in the
midst of a cloud of chiffon, with diamonds, ermine cloaks, and handsome
men waiting for her just offstage. Of course, in reality, it requires a tre-
mendous amount of self-discipline and hard work. But for the child who
dreams of becoming a prima ballerina, Tallulah will make a fine companion
in those early years when the imagination is more graceful than the body.

Tallulah is not delicate looking or princess-like. Indeed, she looks
more like a prize-fighter than a ballerina or a princess. But like most danc-
ers, she is sturdy and strong. When completed, she measures 20 inches tall.
The upper half of her body is made of striped cotton ticking and a sturdy
bright cotton (to suggest leotards) is used for her hips and legs. As you can
see, the pattern for Tallulah's body is split into two basic pieces: the upper
half, above the waist, and the lower half, her hips and legs. Splitting the
pattern in this way allows you to make the body out of two different kinds
of fabric, thus allowing you to suggest clothing without going to the
trouble of actually making them.

Tallulah's chemise is made from colorful flowered cotton and her
skirt is dotted swiss with a taffeta underskirt. Chiffon can be substituted
for the skirt, or satin for the underskirt.

3-1   Tallulah Ballerina

MATERIALS

⅓ yard of striped, print, or plaid medium-weight cotton for the top half of the doll body.

⅓ yard of solid, bright cotton fabric for the legs.

½ yard of white cotton flannel to line the doll.

¼ yard of printed cotton fabric for the chemise.

A rectangle of taffeta or satin, measuring 9 × 17 inches for the underskirt.

A rectangle of dotted swiss, measuring 9 × 17 inches for the skirt.

A piece of felt 8 × 8 inches for her ballet slippers.

Embroidery thread in appropriate colors, for her features, shoe laces, and the straps of the chemise.

3 or 4 yards of mohair yarn for her hair.

A 10-inch piece of lace edging ½-inch wide to trim the lower edge of the chemise.

Two pieces of elastic, each piece ¼-inch wide and 9½-inches long.

Thread to match the fabric and clear nylon thread.

Kapok or Dacron to stuff the doll.

STEP ONE

Enlarge the patterns for Tallulah and her clothes (Fig. 3-2). From the fabrics you have chosen, cut the doll body pieces, the chemise, the skirt, and the underskirt. Be sure to cut the correct number of pieces, as indicated on the patterns. Cut the ballet slippers from felt. Transfer the markings for the eyes, nose, and mouth from the pattern to the *right* side of *one* body piece. Transfer the markings for the laces to the *right* side of one leg piece. Transfer the stitching line, marked down the center of the legs, to the *right* side of *both* leg pieces.

Cut a lining piece for each of the four body pieces. Pin a lining piece to the *wrong* side of each body piece.

STEP TWO

Note: ¼-inch seams are allowed. Unless otherwise stated, stitch fabric with *right* sides together. Remove pins before turning assembled pieces right side out.

Begin by matching together the upper and lower *front* body pieces and the upper and lower *back* pieces. Lay the four body pieces side by side on a flat surface, with the *right* side of the fabric facing *up*. Start with the

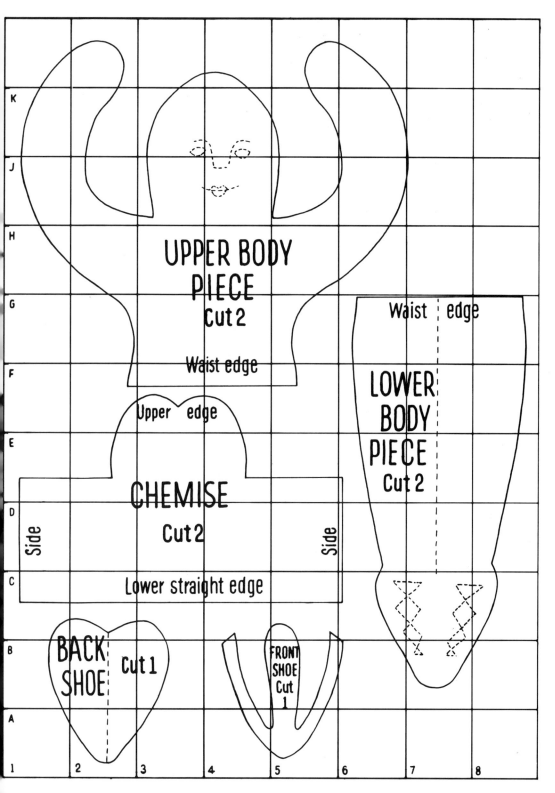

UPPER BODY PIECE
Cut 2

Waist edge

Upper edge

CHEMISE
Cut 2

Side

Side

Lower straight edge

Waist edge

LOWER BODY PIECE
Cut 2

BACK SHOE Cut 1

FRONT SHOE Cut 1

3-2   Tallulah Ballerina

23

upper body piece on which the features are marked and the leg piece on which the lines for shoelaces are marked, and stitch these two pieces together along the waist edge. Next press them flat. This assembled piece is the front of the doll. Now take the remaining unmarked body pieces and

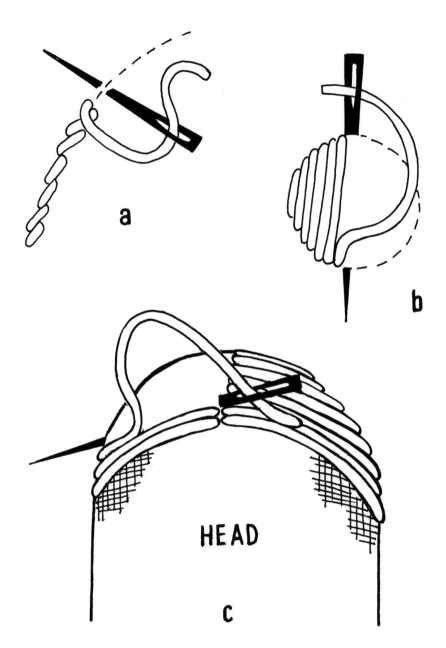

3-3a. Outline or stem embroidery stitch
   b. Satin embroidery stitch
   c. Stitching Tallulah's hair to her head, using the satin stitch

stitch them together along the waist edge. Press them flat. This assembled piece is the back of the doll.

Before proceeding further with the body assembly, the features and the line which creates the illusion of two legs should be embroidered. If your sewing machine has a zigzag stitch, you can use the satin stitch (a series of closely spaced zigzag stitches) for the line on the front and back leg pieces.

If you don't have a zigzag stitch on your machine, you can embroider the line by hand. Use the stem embroidery stitch (Fig. 3-3a). The stem stitch is ideal for lines of color and outlines. Begin from the bottom and work toward the top. Pick up a short vertical stitch diagonally across the line, always keeping the thread on the same side of the needle.

Whether you use a sewing machine or stitch by hand, be sure to use a bright thread that contrasts with the color of the doll's legs. For example: use a blue line on pink legs or a yellow line on navy blue legs.

Tallulah's features are also embroidered. Since they are finely detailed, and unless you are a wizard with your sewing machine, they probably should be embroidered by hand. The stitches are simple; and even if you are not familiar with embroidery, they can be easily mastered. Refer to Fig. 3-3 and practice the stem stitch and the satin stitch on a scrap of fabric before attempting to embroider the doll. The satin stitch is good to use when filling in areas such as the pupils of eyes or the lips. Begin stitching by bringing the needle out on one line; insert the needle through the second line; bring the needle out on the first line, just below the first stitch. When you are ready to try your skill, start with Tallulah's face, and use the stem or outline stitch to embroider along the line which represents her eyebrows and nose. Use the same stitch to outline her eyes. Use the satin stitch to fill in her pupils. Outline her mouth with the stem stitch and fill it in with the satin stitch.

Now, with the *right* sides of the fabric together, align the front of the doll with the back of the doll. Pin the two pieces together, being sure to place the pins in the center of the doll, so as not to interfere with stitching. Next, stitch around the entire perimeter of the pinned pieces, stitching the arms, head, torso, and legs together. Leave a 2-inch opening on one side of the doll. Remove all pins and turn the doll right side out.

STEP THREE

Stuff the ballerina through the opening in her side. Stuff the head first. She need not be stuffed firmly, but push enough stuffing into the curves to give her a smooth, unrumpled outline. After you have stuffed the head, stuff the arms, the toes, the legs, and lastly the torso. When the stuffing is completed, turn ¼ inch of fabric around the open edges to the inside. Stitch the opening securely closed.

STEP FOUR

Tallulah's hair is embroidered to her head. Use mohair yarn and the satin stitch (Fig. 3-3c). Choose an embroidery needle with an eye large enough to thread mohair yarn. Tie a knot at the end of a strand of yarn; then proceed to embroider one half of the front of the doll's head, then the second half. Leave a narrow line of fabric between the two rows of embroidery to simulate a part. Follow the same procedure and embroider the back of the doll's head.

To make the bun at the top of Tallulah's head, cut 3 strands of yarn each 12-inches long. Knot the strands together at one end and braid them. When the braiding is finished, knot the second end. Wrap the braided strand around in a small tight circle and sew it to the top of the doll's head with clear nylon thread.

Begin Tallulah's ballerina slippers by placing a line of satin stitching down the center of the back shoe piece, much as if it were a continuation of the row of stitching down the center back of her legs. Glue this piece to the back of the doll's foot. Glue the front shoe piece to the front of the doll's foot, overlapping slightly the back shoe piece with the front piece. Stitch the front shoe to the back along the sides, using clear nylon thread. Stitch the edges of the shoes to the fabric along all other edges of the leg.

Embroidery thread is used for the laces. The strand of thread for each shoe should be about 20 inches, or long enough so you can tie a bow. Follow the dotted lines transferred from the pattern and stitch the laces to the shoes.

STEP FIVE

Now for Tallulah's clothing. Match the two pieces of the chemise, with *right* sides of the fabric together. Stitch together the lower *straight* edge of both pieces and the upper *curved* edge (Fig. 3-4a). Leave the sides unstitched. Turn the chemise right side out and press. Topstitch the upper, curved edge, placing a row of stitching ⅛ inch inside the outer edge. Stitch a piece of ½-inch wide lace along the lower edge of the chemise. Fold over and sew together the two sides of the chemise, stitching the ends of the lace together as you do so (Fig. 3-4b). Trim the seam to ⅛ inch. Turn the chemise right side out. Slip over the doll's foot and pull it up over her chest, with the bodice in front. Embroider straps to the bodice, run them over the shoulder, and attach them to the back of the chemise. Stitch the chemise to the fabric of the doll's leg at the point where the satin stitching ends in front and in back.

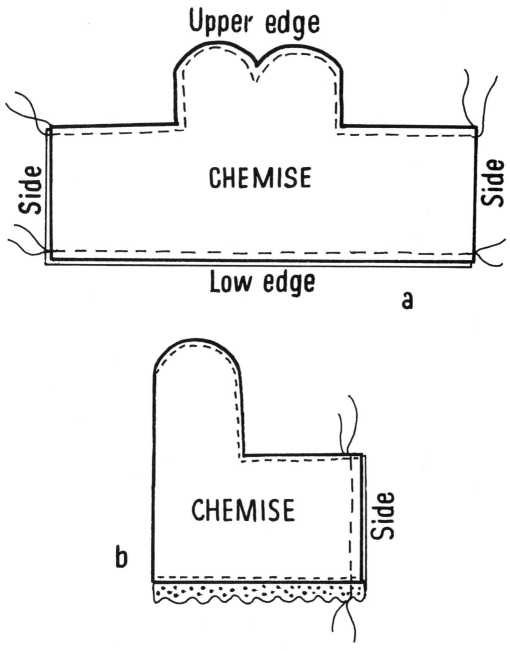

Upper edge

Side

CHEMISE

Side

Low edge

a

b

CHEMISE

Side

3-4a. Stitching together the upper and lower edge of the chemise pieces
   b. Stitching together the sides of the chemise

To make the underskirt, fold the rectangle of taffeta in half, the long narrow way. Stitch the long open edges together, leaving the narrow ends unstitched. Turn the piece right side out and press it. To form a casing for the elastic, run a line of stitching ½ inch inside the stitched edge (Fig. 3-5).

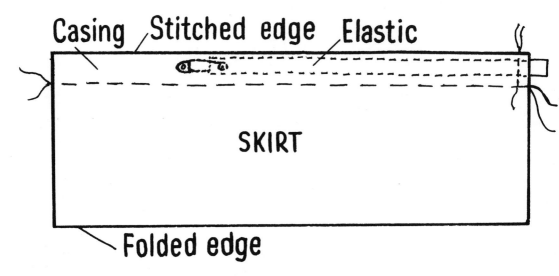

Casing **Stitched edge** **Elastic**

SKIRT

Folded edge

3-5   Stitching the casing and threading the elastic through the casing

Thread the elastic through the casing, then stitch it securely to both ends of the casing. Stitch together the narrow ends of the rectangle, catching in the elastic. Trim the seam to ⅛ inch. Turn the underskirt right side out and slip it on Tallulah.

To make the doll's skirt, follow the same instructions as for the underskirt but substitute a different fabric. When the skirt is completed, slip it over the underskirt.

Tallulah Ballerina is ready to dance.

Chapter 4

Sister Pat and Brother Philly

When the moon rose full in the night sky, Hansel took his little sister by the hand, and together they walked on, guided by the shiny pebbles, which glittered on the ground like silver coins.

Hansel and Gretel
The Brothers Grimm

*T*HERE is a certain tenderness between brother and sister that is sometimes lost in the competitiveness of a brother-brother or a sister-sister relationship. The brother-sister theme seems to crop up consistently in literature, from classics like *War and Peace,* to fairy tales such as *Hansel and Gretel.* Still, if you prefer two brothers or two sisters, or triplets, it only takes a little change in facial expression or clothing to accomplish it.

When completed, Sister Pat and Brother Philly will each measure 16 inches. I think this pair is particularly fun to make. For the jump suits, you can use scraps of fabric or old clothing previously worn by the children who will get the dolls. The bodies can be made from plain or a printed cotton. The shoes are made of black velveteen, but leather-look vinyl will work as well. The jump suits are cut from checked gingham. The heads will be primed with acrylic gesso, painted with acrylic paint, and varnished with a glossy acrylic varnish which gives it a waterproof, nontoxic, and resilient finish.

4-1   Sister Pat and Brother Philly

MATERIALS

1 yard of cotton fabric, printed or plain, for the doll bodies.

1 yard of white cotton flannel to line the doll bodies.

¼ yard of black velveteen, or vinyl, for the shoes.

½ yard of suitable cotton for the jump suits.

Scraps of yarn for laces and shoulder ties.

Acrylic gesso, acrylic paint in various colors, and acrylic glossy varnish for the head, hair, and features. Check labels to be sure the brand of paint you buy is *nontoxic* when dry.

Thread to match fabric and clear nylon thread.

Kapok or Dacron to stuff the dolls.

STEP ONE

Enlarge the patterns for the two dolls and their clothes (Figs. 4-2 and 4-3). From the fabric you have chosen, cut the appropriate number of pieces for the doll bodies, their shoes, and their jump suits. Transfer the dotted line that is marked across the neck to the *right* side of the fabric. Do *not* transfer the markings for the face and features to the fabric yet. Transfer all other markings to the *wrong* side of the fabric.

Cut lining pieces for the doll bodies and the shoes. Pin these pieces to the *wrong* side of the corresponding pieces.

STEP TWO

Note: ¼-inch seams are allowed. Unless otherwise stated, stitch fabric with *right* sides together. Remove all pins from the fabric before turning the assembled pieces right side out.

To begin, a shoe piece has to be stitched to the end of each of the eight legs: to do this, first pin one shoe piece to one leg piece, with right sides of the fabric together (Fig. 4-4). Stitch the straight edges together. Press each assembled piece so that shoe and body are flat.

Place a *front* and a *back* body piece together, aligning them so that legs, arms, and heads match. Now pin or baste the pieces in this position, so you can sew them together without the pieces slipping on the machine. Stitch around the entire perimeter of the doll, leaving an opening between the X's marked on the side. Repeat basting and stitching procedures for the second doll.

Turn both dolls right side out through the opening in their sides.

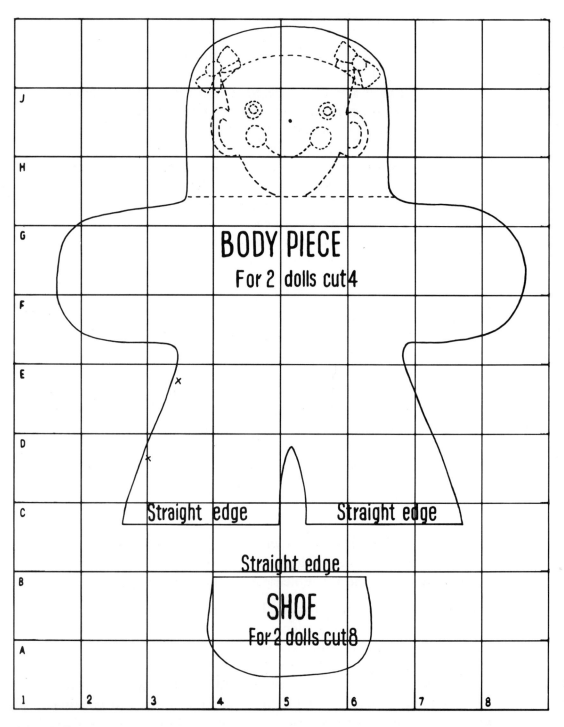

BODY PIECE
For 2 dolls cut 4

Straight edge   Straight edge

Straight edge

SHOE
For 2 dolls cut 8

4-2   Doll pattern

32

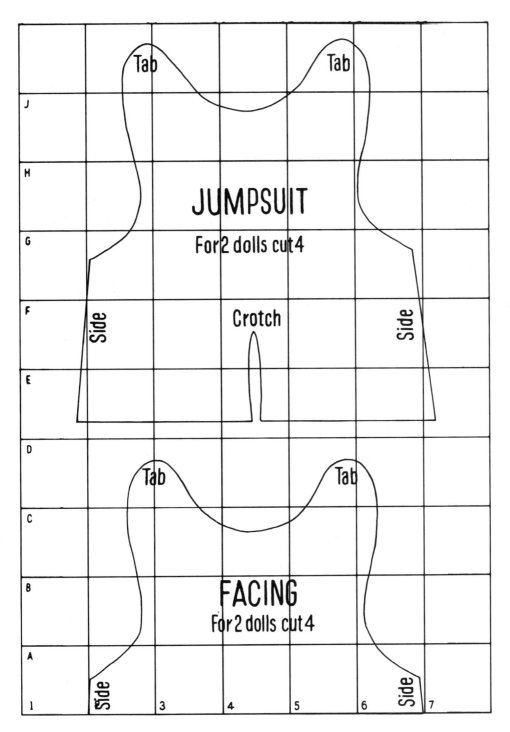

4-3 Clothing pattern

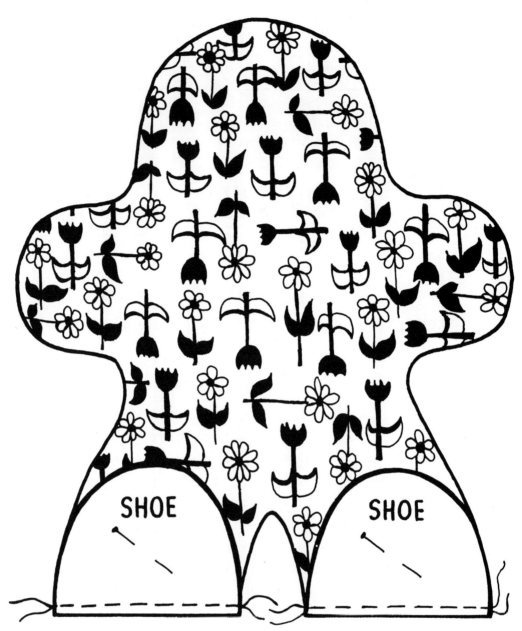

4-4   Stitching the shoes to the body

STEP THREE

It requires a little care to stuff a doll where the head and body are one piece. Simple shapes can be deceptive; and if they are not stuffed uniformly, wrinkles will result at the base of the neck and limbs. Stuff each doll slowly. First fill out the curves around the edge of the head. Then fill the center of the head. To achieve a smoother overall appearance, use *small* amounts of stuffing rather than large handfuls: use wads of stuffing approximately the size of a fifty-cent piece. After the head is finished, stuff the arms, then the shoes and legs. Lastly, stuff the center body cavity. Fill the dolls until they are full, yet squeezably soft. Over-stuffing causes bulging and strains the seams.

After the toy is stuffed, turn ¼ inch of fabric to the inside, around the edges. Stitch this opening shut, by hand, using clear nylon thread.

STEP FOUR

The hair and the faces for these dolls are painted on with acrylics. Most acrylic paints and varnishes are nontoxic when dry, but I strongly recommend that you check the labels to be sure that they are marked nontoxic, especially if the dolls are intended for children at an age where they put things in their mouth.

To begin work on the heads, first paint the entire surface of each head to the dotted lines at the neck with acrylic gesso. The gesso creates a smooth white, nonabsorbent surface for the paint. If paint is applied directly to the fabric, it will soak into the stuffing and the colors will lose their brilliance. Let the gesso dry thoroughly, overnight if possible.

When the gesso has dried, transfer the markings for the outline of the face to this covered surface. These markings are transferred from the pattern to the head in the same way markings are transferred from a pattern to fabric. You can paint the face and neck pink, yellow, brown, or any color you have in mind. Choose an appropriate contrasting color for the hair. Allow the paint sufficient time to dry.

Now transfer the markings for the features from the pattern to the face. The face on the pattern is a girl, omit the bows and paint a shorter hair style for the boy doll. Paint the pupils of the eye black, then add a white highlight. The nose, the mouth, and the line inside each ear can be painted red, orange, or pink. The cheeks should be painted a slightly darker shade than the color of the face. You can paint the bows in the girl's hair in a color that corresponds with her clothing. Last of all, outline in contrasting colors the face, the hairline, the eyes, the boy's neck, and the girl's bows. Bright blue goes well with a pink face and dark hair; yellow or orange goes well with brown. Run slender lines of contrasting color through the hair to suggest texture. Allow the paint to dry.

Now the heads should be varnished with acrylic gloss. A coat of varnish not only enhances the colors and gives a shiny sparkly appearance, but also waterproofs. Varnish the entire painted surface of each doll and set them aside to dry.

STEP FIVE

Note: ¼-inch seams allowed.

Sister Pat and Brother Philly are dressed in matching jump suits. Begin with the first pair. Align the front and back jump suit pieces. With *right* sides of the fabric together, stitch the crotch seam. Next, stitch both side seams from the armhole opening to the base of the leg.

Stitch the side seams of the two facing pieces. Turn ¼ inch of fabric along the lower edge of the facing to the inside. Press and then stitch this hem in place.

Turn the jump suit right side out. Pin the *right* side of the facing to the *right* side of the jump suit. Match the tabs and armhole edges as exactly as possible (Fig. 4-5). Baste and then stitch the facing to the jump suit. Trim the seam to ⅛ inch. Turn the facing to the inside and tack the hem of the facing to the jump suit at the side seams. Press the jump suit.

Try the jump suit on a doll, then turn the trouser legs up to a suitable length and pin them in place. Remove the jump suit and hem by hand.

Replace the jump suit on a doll and tie the shoulder tabs together with a bow of bright yarn, stitched through the fabric with a sharp embroidery needle.

Repeat the above procedures for the second jump suit.

Sister Pat and Brother Philly are ready to play. If you like them, why not make an entire family: Mom and Dad, Grandma and Grandpa, Aunt and Uncle. Make the dolls the same way, just paint different faces and alter the clothing.

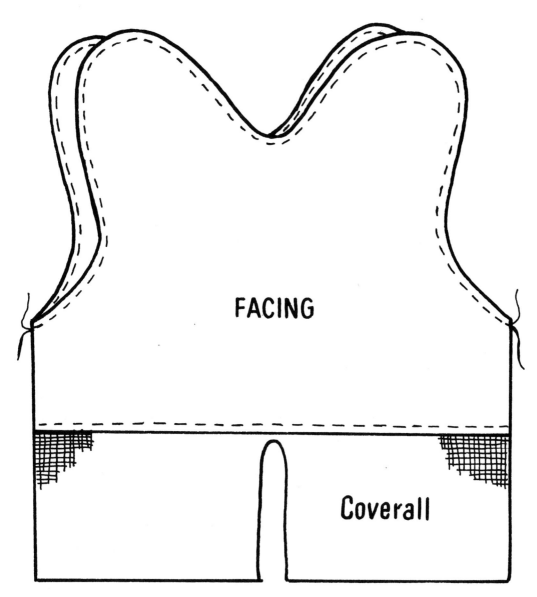

FACING

Coverall

4-5   Stitching the facing to the coverall

Chapter 5

Kronkite Clown

Simple Simon met a pieman,
    Going to the fair;
Says Simple Simon to the pieman,
    "Let me taste your ware."

Says the pieman to Simple Simon,
    "Show me first your penny;"
Says Simple Simon to the pieman,
    "Indeed, I have not any."

Simple Simon
Traditional Nursery Rhyme

CLOWNS, with their slapstick behavior, their strange shapeless dress, big shoes, and floppy hats, appeal immensely to children. The clown, the jester, the simpleton, and the dwarf have an ancient history: they were companions to kings and queens. Not only their comic entertainment, but their bumbling, silly antics and disordered view of a situation often gave insights and solutions to difficult problems.

Although Kronkite Clown appears elaborate, he is relatively easy to make. When completed, he will measure 22 inches tall and will be able to stand on his own two feet. You can go to town with color combinations for his dress and can substitute any number of funny faces if the one shown doesn't appeal to your sense of the ridiculous. His ruff, hat, and legs are cut from splashy cotton prints. His upper body is pink brushed denim; a sturdy fabric, yet soft to the touch, that comes in a wide range of colors. Kronkite's shirt is bonded panne velvet, which adds considerable sparkle to his personality, but velvet or velveteen will work almost as well as an alternate fabric.

5-1 Kronkite Clown

MATERIALS

½ yard of sturdy cotton fabric for the legs, hat, and ruff.

½ yard of crisp pink fabric for the upper half of the body and the ears.

1 yard of white cotton flannel to line the doll.

⅓ yard of a glossy fabric for the shirt.

Two 2 ounce skeins of Orlon® yarn in contrasting colors for the pompoms.

3 or 4 yards of bright rug yarn for his hair.

4 × 5-inch piece of white felt for the face mask.

9 × 12-inch piece of black felt for the soles of the feet.

Various scraps of colored felt for the features.

A clean, empty plastic bottle to cut lining for the soles.

Single fold bias tape 1-inch wide to use for a casing in the shirt sleeves.

An 11-inch long by ¼-inch wide strip of elastic for the ruff, and two 7-inch lengths for the sleeves.

One snap closure for the shirt neck.

Thread to match fabric and clear nylon thread.

Kapok or Dacron to stuff the doll.

STEP ONE

Enlarge the patterns for Kronkite and his clothes (Figs. 5-2 and 5-3). From the fabric you have chosen, cut the appropriate number of pieces to represent his body and his clothes, as marked on the patterns. Transfer the marking for the face mask to the *right* side of *one* head piece. Transfer the markings for the features to the face mask. Transfer the stitching lines for the fingers to the *right* side of the hands. Transfer all other markings to the *wrong* side of the fabric.

Cut linings for all pieces of the doll body. Pin the lining fabric to the *wrong* side of each corresponding piece.

Using the pattern for the sole of the foot, cut two soles from the plastic bottle. Trim ¼ inch from the perimeter of the plastic pieces.

STEP TWO

Note: ½-inch seams allowed. Unless otherwise stated, stitch fabric with *right* sides together. Remove all pins before turning assembled pieces right side out.

To begin, take the *upper* body piece that is marked with *dotted lines* for the face mask and stitch it along the waist edge to one *lower* body

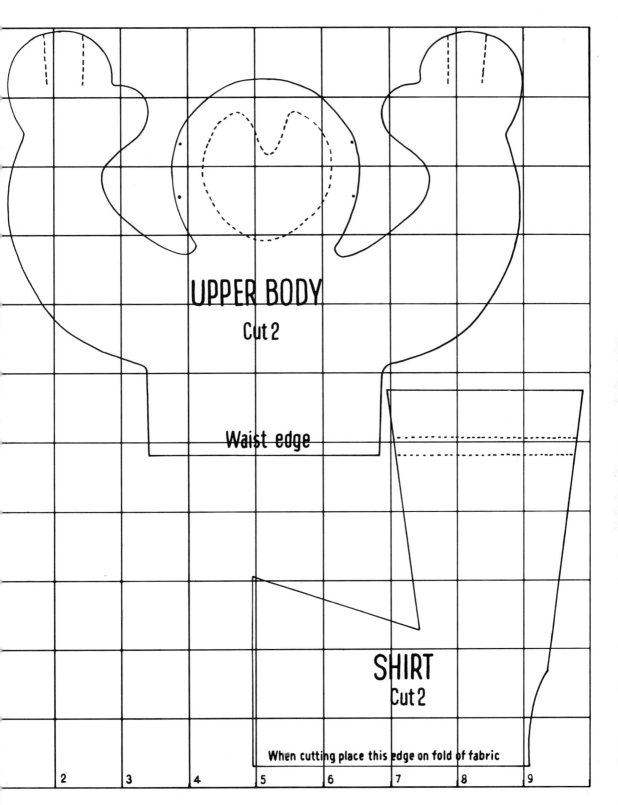

UPPER BODY

Cut 2

Waist edge

SHIRT

Cut 2

When cutting place this edge on fold of fabric

| 2 | 3 | 4 | 5 | 6 | 7 | 8 | 9 |

First part of doll and clothing

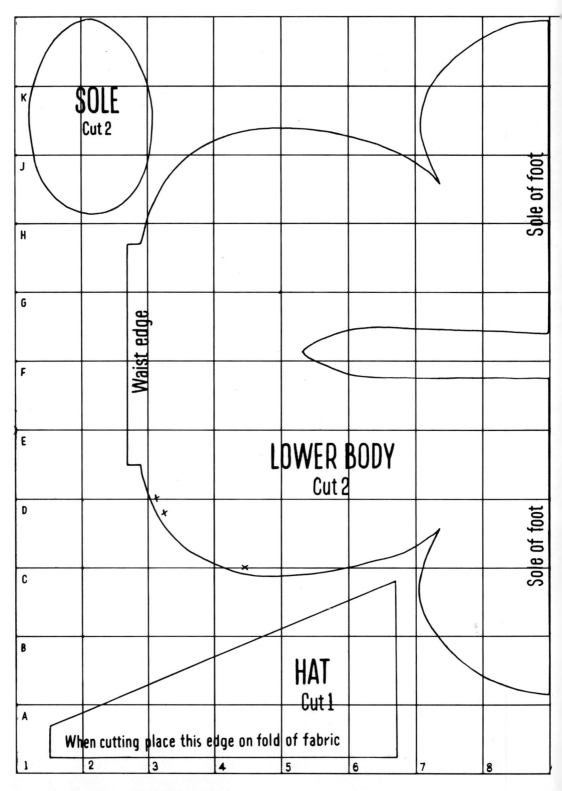

SOLE
Cut 2

LOWER BODY
Cut 2

Waist edge

Sole of foot

Sole of foot

HAT
Cut 1

When cutting place this edge on fold of fabric

5-3   Second part of doll and clothing

42

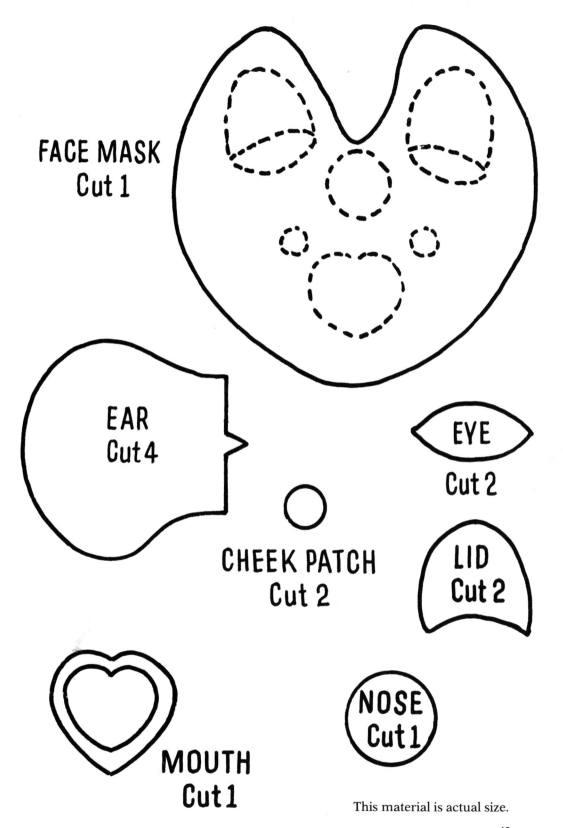

FACE MASK
Cut 1

EAR
Cut 4

EYE
Cut 2

CHEEK PATCH
Cut 2

LID
Cut 2

NOSE
Cut 1

MOUTH
Cut 1

This material is actual size.

piece. Next, stitch the *unmarked* upper body piece to the remaining *lower* body piece. Press each of these two assembled pieces flat.

The ears are next. First, stitch together each pair of ear pieces, leaving the *notched* edge *open*. Turn the ears right side out and press. If you have trouble turning small pieces right side out, try using tweezers. Now topstitch ¼ inch from the perimeter of each ear, leaving the *notched* edge *open*. Pin an ear between the two sets of dots marked on each side of the head (Fig. 5-4). Pin the ears to the *right* side of the fabric. The *notched* edge of the ear should extend ½ inch beyond the seamline. Baste each ear in place.

With right sides together, align the two body pieces so that the hands, head, legs, and feet match, then baste or pin them together. Stitch around the entire perimeter of the body, leaving unstitched the area between the two X's marked on the side of one leg and between the soles of the feet (Fig. 5-4). Turn the doll right side out through the opening in his side.

To stitch the soles to the clown's feet, first turn ½ inch of fabric to the inside around the base of one foot. Place a plastic sole in the foot opening so that it forms a flat, sole-like surface. If the plastic does not fit correctly into the opening, trim to fit. Now place a felt sole over the plastic sole and trim if necessary. Stitch the felt sole to the fabric, by hand, using clear nylon thread (see Fig. 6-6a). Use an overcast stitch for this purpose (diagonal stitches over the two edges, spaced evenly apart and at a uniform depth). Stitch around the perimeter of the foot twice. Now stitch the second sole to the other foot.

To create the illusion of fingers, topstitch with your sewing machine or embroider by hand along the stitching lines indicated on each hand.

STEP THREE

The clown is stuffed through the opening in his thigh. Stuff the head first, *firmly* filling out the curves. Next stuff the hands, pushing *tiny* amounts of stuffing between the stitching lines to fill out the fingers. The blunt end of an aluminum crochet hook is often helpful for pushing stuffing into small areas.

Stuff the feet and ankles *firmly,* so that the stuffing will not settle or shift; otherwise the clown will not stand when you are finished.

STEP FOUR

Hair and features are next, an important step in determining Kronkite's character. Depending on how you place his features, he can be a happy clown or a sad one.

Use rug yarn for the hair. Cut 3 or 4 yards of it into uneven lengths, measuring 2, 4, and 6 inches. Take a sharp needle with a large eye and

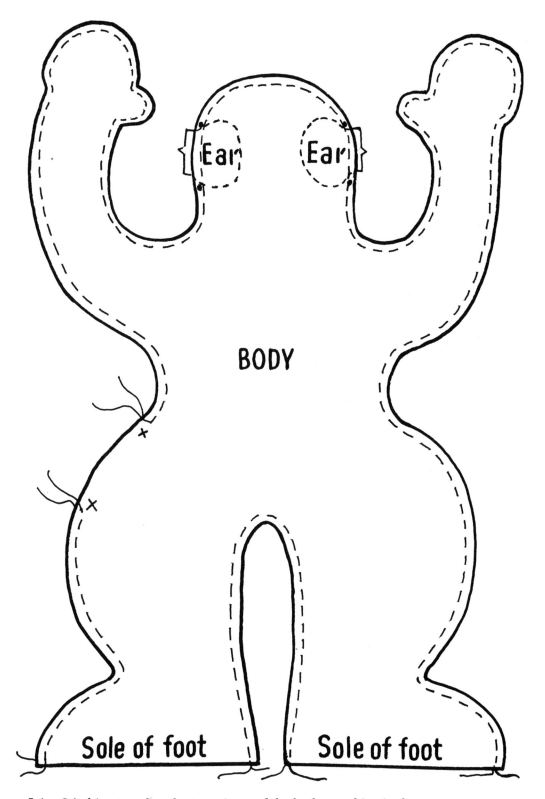

BODY

Ear Ear

Sole of foot   Sole of foot

5-4   Stitching together the two pieces of the body, catching in the ears

thread it with one of the shorter pieces of yarn. Attach the yarn to the head, so that there is an equal length of yarn on each side of the point where the needle penetrates the fabric. Start just above and in front of the ear, by the ear-to-ear seamline. Remove the needle and tie the yarn in a knot so that you have two strands of approximately equal length (see Fig. 15-6). Stitch a full row of the shorter strands of yarn along the seamline that runs between the ears. These short strands should fall forward over the face to form bangs. Now stitch a second row of yarn, using 4-inch and 6-inch lengths of yarn, and place it on the back of the head, halfway down and ear to ear. Fill in the area between the two rows with the remaining strands of yarn, alternating the lengths to suit your fancy. You can trim and shape the hair when you're finished, but I think Kronkite's personality calls for a shock of unkempt hair.

A clown's face is his calling card. I've given Kronkite a happy face. Glue the face mask to the head, and the features to the face mask at the points indicated. Glue tiny triangular pieces of white felt to the dark lower portions of the eye for highlights. When the glue is dry, sew the face mask and the features to the head, stitching around the perimeter of each piece with clear nylon thread.

If you want a different face, silly or sad or whatever, simply draw your concept of the face on a piece of paper, cut the features from felt, then try a few combinations on the doll's face until you get it just right. When you're satisfied, then glue the features and stitch as above.

STEP FIVE

You need 6 pompoms to trim Kronkite's hat, shoes, and shirt. They are made from yarn. Use as many different colors as you can. Pompoms are easy to make. I first learned how to make them for my ice skates when I was a teenager and then again when pompom dolls were the vogue. First cut a piece of cardboard 2-inches wide and 6-inches long. Wrap the yarn around the piece of cardboard 35 or 40 times (Fig. 5-5). Slip the yarn off the cardboard and tie it tightly in the center with another strand of yarn. Clip both ends of the yarn open. Fluff the yarn into a ball with your fingers.

To attach the pompoms to the fabric, stitch a piece of yarn through the fabric and then through the center of the pompom. Tie the yarn in a knot. Attach a pompom to each of the clown's shoes and set the remaining pompoms aside. They will be attached to the clothing later.

STEP SIX

Note: ¼-inch seams allowed.

Kronkite wears a shirt, hat, and ruff; the bright fabric from which the lower half of his body is made also serves as his trousers. Start with his

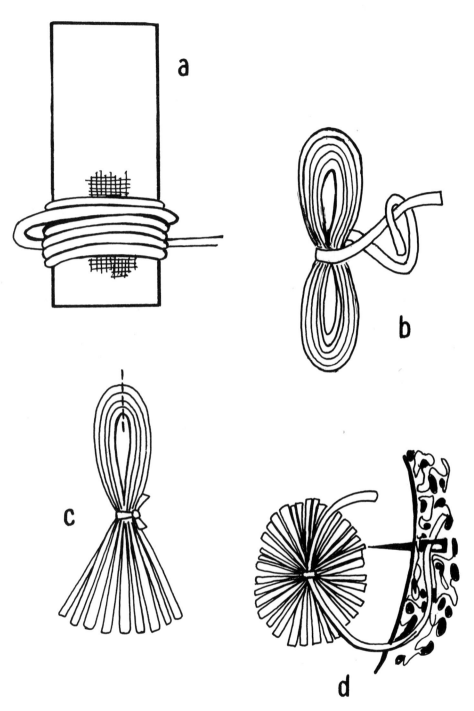

5-5a. Wrapping the yarn around the cardboard
   b. Tying the center of the yarn after removing it from the cardboard
   c. Clipping the ends of the tied yarn
   d. Attaching the pompom to the fabric

shirt. Stitch the shoulder seams of the two shirt pieces together, from the neck edge to the tips of the sleeves. Cut a slit approximately 2-inches long down the center back from the neck edge. Turn ¼ inch of fabric to the inside, along the slit edges and around the neck edge. Press and stitch this turned edge by machine or hand.

Open out each of the sleeves. Press the shoulder seam open. Hem the ends of the sleeves by turning ¼ inch of fabric to the inside along the raw edge. Press and stitch the folded edge in place. Observe the dotted lines which are marked on the *wrong* side of the fabric just above the sleeve hem, and cut a 1-inch wide strip of single fold bias tape to match the width of the open sleeves, then place it over the dotted lines. The *wrong* side of the tape and the *wrong* side of the fabric should be together. Pin the tape to the sleeve, and place the pins down the center of the tape. To form a casing for the elastic, stitch close to both edges of the tape. Thread a 7-inch length of ¼-inch wide elastic through each casing. Stitch the elastic to the fabric at both ends of the casing.

Stitch both underarm seams from the tip of the sleeve to the lower edge of the shirt. Try the shirt on the doll and turn up a suitable hem. Stitch the hem in place. Press the shirt.

Attach a snap closure to the shirt neck edge. Stitch two pompoms to the center front of the shirt. Put the shirt on Kronkite.

To make his ruff, begin by pressing the rectangular piece of fabric in half, right sides together, so that you have a *long narrow* piece. Stitch together the long *straight* edges opposite the fold, leaving the *narrow* ends open. Turn the piece right side out and press. To form a casing for the elastic, run a line of stitching ½ inch inside the stitched edge of the piece (see Fig. 3-5). Topstitch ¼ inch inside the opposite edge (you can make topstitching more decorative with zigzag stitches and contrasting colors of thread). Now thread an 11-inch length of ¼-inch wide elastic through the casing. Stitch the elastic to the fabric at each end of the casing.

Stitch the narrow ends of the rectangle together. Trim the seam. Place the ruff on the clown, elastic around his neck. Place the seam at the back of the neck, turned to the inside so it doesn't show.

Fold the triangular hat piece in half. Stitch together the side of the hat opposite the fold, then stitch across the top of the hat (Fig. 15-8). Trim the seam. Turn ¼ inch of fabric along the base of the hat to the inside and stitch it in place. Turn the hat right side out and press. Stitch two pompoms to the tip of the hat and stitch the hat to the doll's head.

Kronkite Clown is ready to join the circus.

Chapter 6

Timothy Dragon

> ...a drop or two of Dragon's blood gives courage, invulnerability, and magical understanding.
>
> *The Glass Harmonica*
> Barbara Ninde Byfield

*T*HE dragon is a guardian of pathways, gates, and treasures. In medieval times, he was the creature most often chosen to test a knight's courage. He was a formidable test, breathing fire and smoke; he had sharp claws and a lashing tail and his body was protected by an armour plate of scales. In bestiaries, the dragon was defined as the "biggest of all serpents, in fact of all living things on earth."

I like to think of dragons as guardians of small children, creatures who keep nightmares and cold winds away. Timothy Dragon is this kind of dragon. His body is cut from flower-printed cotton fabrics, three different but compatible prints. The fins that run down his back are cut from brightly colored felt. When completed, Timothy Dragon will measure 12 inches tall and 17 inches long.

MATERIALS

⅓ yard each of three different medium-weight printed cotton fabrics for the body, belly, and ears.

½ yard of white cotton flannel for the lining.

Scraps of felt in three colors for the fins and scraps of felt for the eyes.

9 × 12-inch piece of black felt for the soles of the feet.

Kapok or Dacron for stuffing.

A clean, empty plastic bottle.

Thread to match the fabric and clear nylon thread.

6-1   Timothy Dragon

STEP ONE

Enlarge the pattern for Timothy Dragon (Fig. 6-2). Cut the appropriate number of body, belly, strip, and ear pieces from the fabrics you have chosen. Transfer all markings to the *wrong* side of the fabric.

Cut lining pieces for the body, belly, and ears of the dragon. Pin each lining piece to the *wrong* side of its corresponding body piece.

Cut 12 fins from the pieces of felt, four of each color. Cut the pupils and eyes and two small triangular pieces of white felt for highlights. Cut the soles of the feet from black felt.

Cut 4 soles and 2 ears from the plastic bottle. Trim these pieces ¼ inch *smaller* than the pattern pieces.

STEP TWO

> *Note:* ¼-inch seams allowed. Unless otherwise stated, stitch fabric with *right* sides together. Remove all pins before turning assembled pieces right side out.

Begin the dragon's body by stitching together the *long, straight* edge of the two belly pieces. Press the assembled piece flat. Stitch the breast strip to the belly piece, between the two dots (Fig. 6-3).

With right sides of the fabric together, align the legs and tail of half the belly piece with the legs and tail of one body piece (Fig. 6-4). Stitch from the tip of the tail between the X's marked on the body piece, to the X beneath the chin, leaving the base of the legs *open*. Align the remaining half of the belly with the other body piece and stitch between the X's as above.

Stitch the head and neck of the dragon together, from the point where the breast strip joins beneath the head to the dot marked on the upperside at the base of the neck (Fig. 6-5).

Insert the fins between the body pieces, alternating colors every second or third fin (Fig. 6-5). Stitch the body pieces together, catching in the fins.

Stitch together the tail to the tip.

Stitch the inner ear to the outer ear, leaving the base open. Repeat the procedure and assemble the second ear. Turn the ears right side out.

STEP THREE

Turn the dragon right side out through the belly opening. Next turn ¼ inch of fabric to the inside, around the opening at the base of one leg. Fit one of the plastic soles you cut from the plastic bottle into the opening (Fig. 6-6a). Now place a felt sole over the plastic sole and hand stitch the felt sole to the base of the leg, using clear nylon thread. To ensure durability, stitch around the perimeter twice. Now repeat this procedure for the three remaining legs.

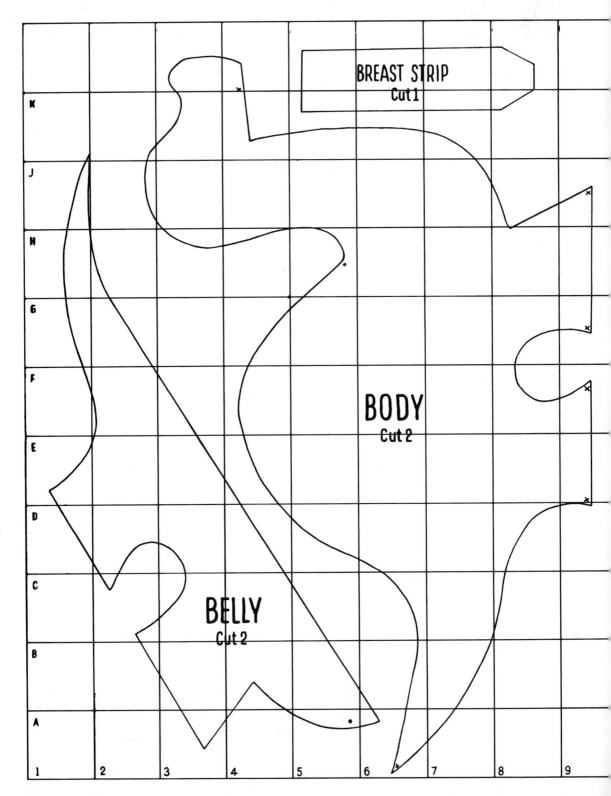

BREAST STRIP
Cut 1

BODY
Cut 2

BELLY
Cut 2

6-2   Timothy Dragon

52

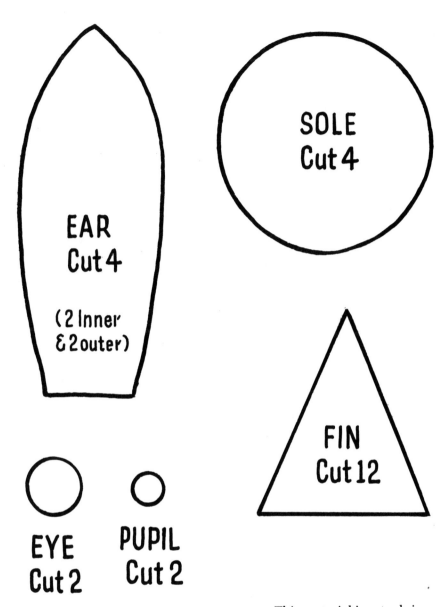

EAR
Cut 4

(2 Inner
& 2 outer)

SOLE
Cut 4

FIN
Cut 12

EYE
Cut 2

PUPIL
Cut 2

This material is actual size.

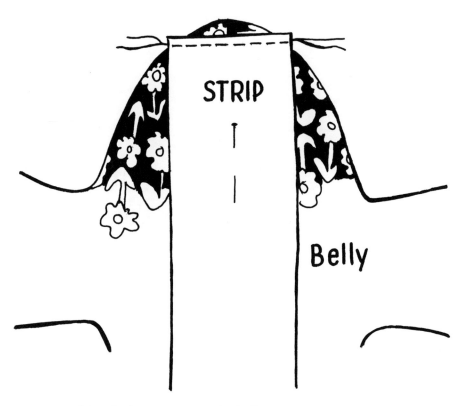

6-3   Stitching the breast strip to the belly

STEP FOUR

Firmly stuff Timothy Dragon through the opening in his belly with kapok or Dacron. Stuff the head and neck first, then the legs and tail, and
lastly the center body cavity. Turn ¼ inch of fabric to the inside, along the
edges of the belly slit. Stitch the slit shut with clear nylon thread. Now,
take a tuck and stitch the inside of each leg to the belly. This aligns the legs
so that the toy will stand with more stability.

STEP FIVE

Timothy Dragon is easy to finish. First slip the plastic supports into
his ears and turn ¼ inch of fabric to the inside, along the opening. Next
stitch the opening shut. Pinch the base of an ear together and stitch it shut
(Fig. 6-6b), then stitch the ear to the head. Repeat for the other ear.
    Glue the highlights to the eyes and the eyes to the head with liquid
latex or a cloth glue. Stitch around the eyes with clear nylon thread.
    Timothy Dragon is now complete and ready to stand guard.

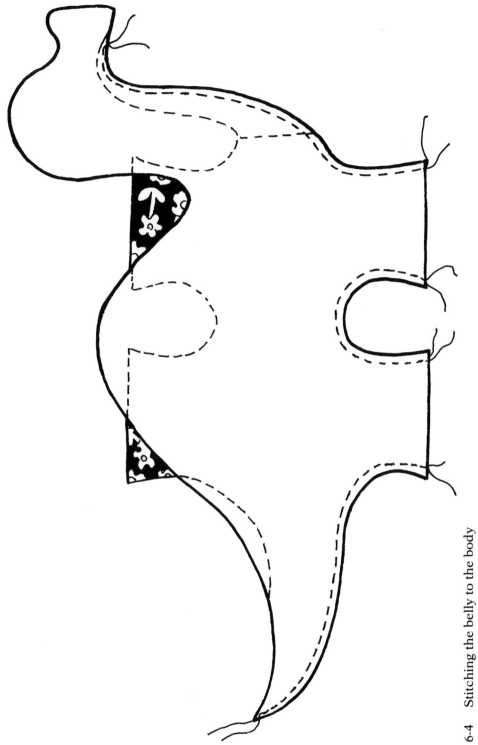

6-4 Stitching the belly to the body

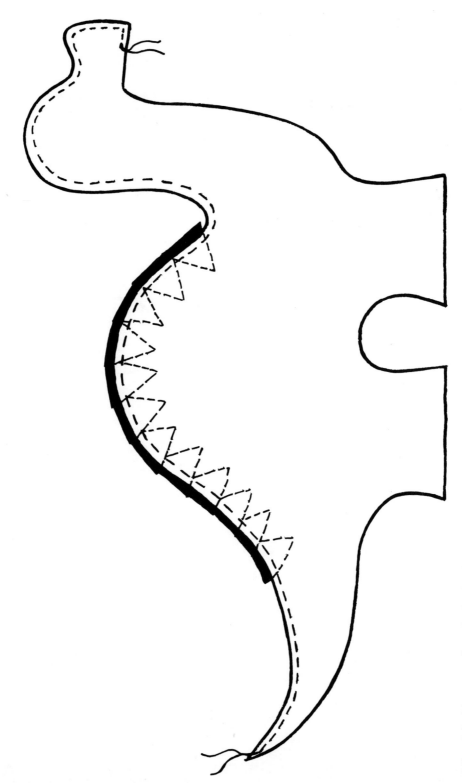

6-5   Stitching together the body pieces, catching in the fins

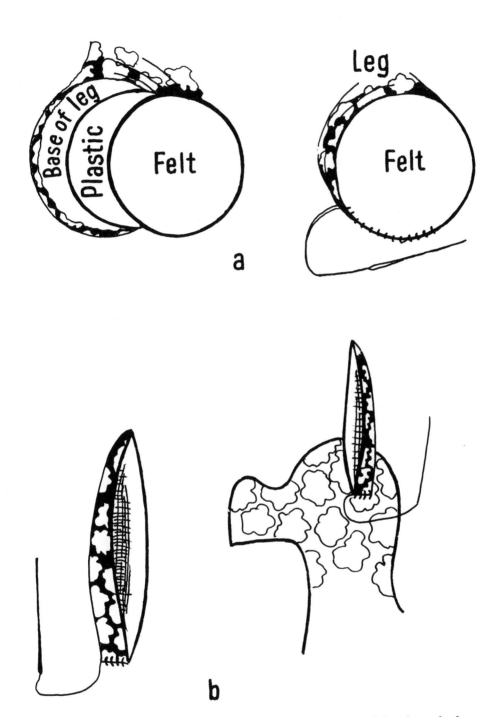

6-6a. Placing a felt sole over a plastic sole and stitching the felt sole to the base of the leg
   b. Pinching the base of the ear together and stitching the ear to the head

Chapter 7

Elmo Elephant

Elephants do not gallop. They move
from places at varying rates of speed. If
an elephant wished to catch an express
train he could not gallop, but he could
catch the train.

Moti Guj—Mutineer
Rudyard Kipling

*E*LEPHANTS are fascinating creatures. They are very intelligent and really do have excellent memories. They are affectionate, loyal, and devoted. Their ancestors, the mammoths, walked the earth more than 50 million years ago. Today two branches of the elephant family remain: the African and the Indian. African elephants have larger ears than the Indian variety and grow to a height of 11 feet at the shoulders. Their tusks may measure 11 feet in length. Indian elephants are slightly smaller and have better dispositions. Elephants are vegetarians and some live to be 60 years old.

Because his ears are large, Elmo Elephant is more of the African variety than the Indian. His body is cut from sturdy, bright flower-printed cotton fabric, either duck or sailcloth. The lining for his belly is either taffeta or satin. His tail and collar are made from rug yarn. His eyes, soles of the feet, and the end of his trunk are felt. When completed he will measure 10 × 10 inches.

7-1   Elmo Elephant

MATERIALS

½ yard of sturdy cotton for the body, head, gusset, and
    outer ears.

½ yard of white cotton flannel to line the elephant.

⅓ yard of satin or taffeta for the belly and the inner
    ears.

A 9 × 12-inch rectangle of black felt for the soles of the
    feet and the pupils. A small piece of pink felt for
    the end of the trunk. A scrap of bright green or
    blue felt for the eyes.

3 or 4 yards of bright rug yarn for the tail and collar.

A clean, empty plastic bottle, ½-gallon or gallon size, to
    cut out pieces to support the ears and the soles of
    the feet.

A wire clothes hanger for leg supports.

Kapok or Dacron to stuff the elephant.

Thread to match the fabric and clear nylon thread.

STEP ONE

Enlarge the patterns for the elephant (Fig. 7-2). From the fabrics you
have chosen, cut the appropriate number of pieces as marked on the pattern. Transfer the dotted lines and the X's to the *right* side of each head
piece. Transfer the other markings to the *wrong* side of the fabric.

Cut lining pieces for the body, head, gusset, inner ears, and outer ears.
Pin the lining to the *wrong* side of each corresponding piece.

Use the pattern for the ear as a guide and cut two ears from the plastic
bottle. Trim ½ inch of plastic from the perimeter of each ear. Use the sole
patterns as a guide and cut two front feet and two back feet from the plastic bottle. Trim ¼ inch of plastic from the perimeter of each foot. Use the
nose pattern as a guide and cut a plastic circle for the end of the trunk,
then trim ¼ inch from the perimeter.

STEP TWO

> *Note:* ¼-inch seams allowed. Unless otherwise stated, stitch fab-
> ric with *right* sides together. Remove all pins before turning as-
> sembled pieces right side out.

Elmo's head and body are made separately in two individual parts.
After they are stuffed, they are positioned and then stitched together. This
way, the head can be sewn on the body at a variety of angles and several
different elephants can be made from the same pattern, each with its own
personality.

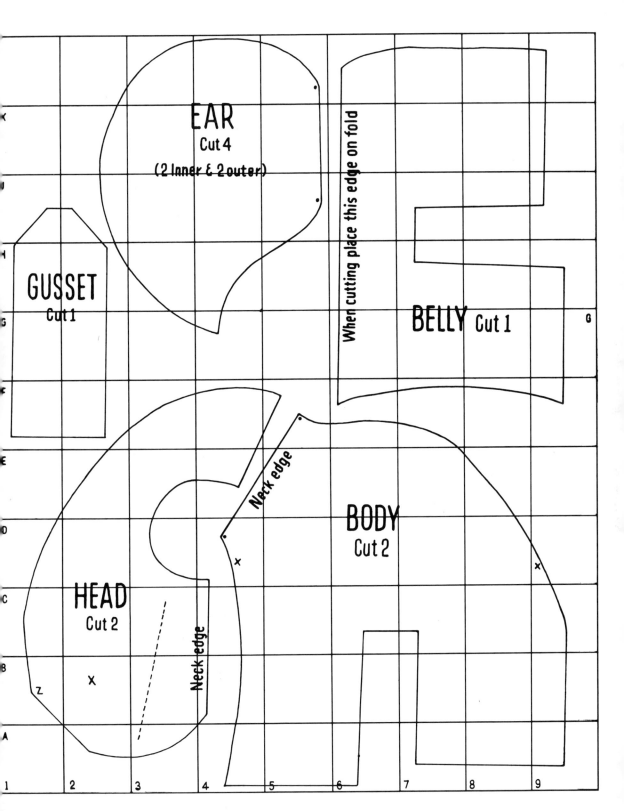

EAR
Cut 4
(2 inner & 2 outer)

GUSSET
Cut 1

When cutting place this edge on fold

BELLY Cut 1

Neck edge

BODY
Cut 2

HEAD
Cut 2

Neck edge

-2   Elmo Elephant

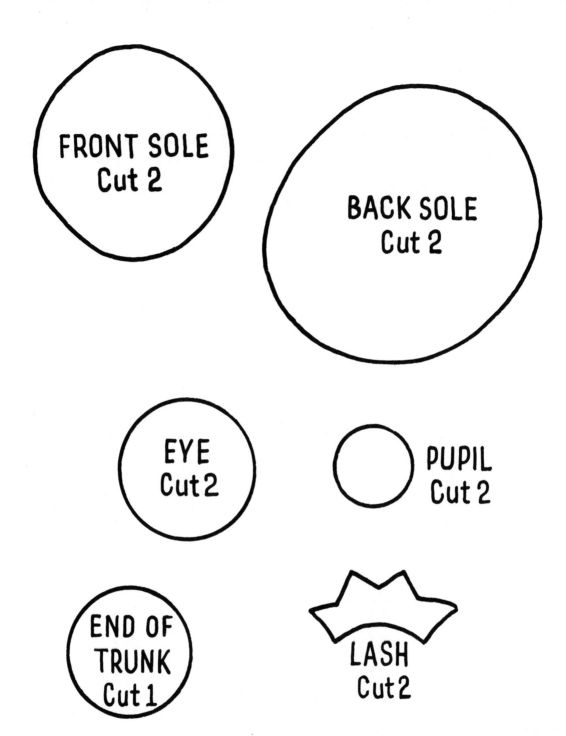

FRONT SOLE
Cut 2

BACK SOLE
Cut 2

EYE
Cut 2

PUPIL
Cut 2

END OF
TRUNK
Cut 1

LASH
Cut 2

This material is actual size.

Start by stitching Elmo's belly to his body. First align a front and back leg on the belly piece with the legs of *one* body piece, *right* sides of the fabric together. Pin or baste the two pieces together from the X marked on the body piece above the rear hind leg to the X marked above the front leg; then stitch the two pieces together (Fig. 7-3a). Follow the same instructions and stitch the front and rear leg of the second body piece to the remaining half of the belly piece.

Look carefully at Fig. 7-3a and note how the backs of the two body pieces are stitched together. Stitch the back together from the X marked where the belly is joined above the rear hind leg to the dot marked at the tip of the neck. Stitch the underside of the neck together from the X marked above the front legs to the dot marked at the neck edge. Leave the neck edge open. Turn this piece right side out and set it aside.

To stitch Elmo's head, start with the inner curve of the two trunk pieces and stitch from the tip of the trunk to the neck edge (Fig. 7-3b). Next, stitch together the opposite, outer side of the trunk, from the tip to the point marked X. The tip of the gusset is joined to the head at this point. To determine how the gusset is attached, first take another look at Fig. 7-3b, then baste the gusset to the head, placing the tip at the point marked X and stitching the gusset to one side of the head. Ease the gusset to fit the curves of the head. Machine stitch the gusset to the side of the head. Baste and stitch the gusset to the other side of the head. Turn the head right side out. The neck edge will be open.

To make an ear, attach one *inner* ear piece to one *outer* ear piece, stitching around the perimeter, but leaving an opening between the two dots marked on the ear fabric. Turn each ear right side out and press.

STEP THREE

Here, a felt sole is sewn into the base of each leg and a felt circle is sewn over the open end of the trunk. To begin, turn ¼ inch of fabric to the inside, around the opening at the base of one leg. Fit the plastic sole into the opening so that it forms a flat surface and covers the base of the leg (Fig. 6-6a). If the plastic piece is too large, trim it to fit. Place a black felt sole over the plastic sole. This piece should also be trimmed for an accurate fit. Stitch the felt to the fabric at the base of the leg. Use clear nylon thread and an overcast stitch here, stitching twice around the base of each leg to be certain the sole is secure. Repeat this procedure for each of the three remaining legs. Then follow the same instructions and stitch the pink felt circle to the end of the trunk.

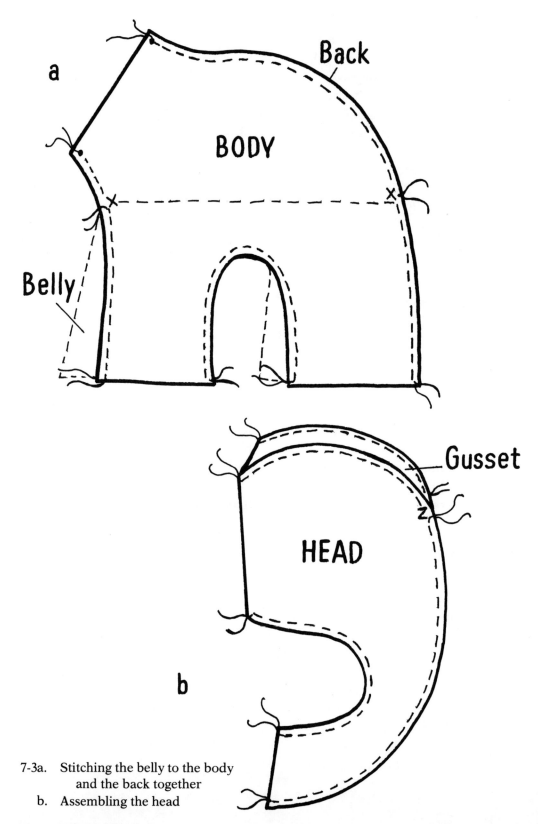

a

Back

BODY

Belly

HEAD

Gusset

b

7-3a. Stitching the belly to the body
and the back together
b. Assembling the head

STEP FOUR

Before you can stuff the elephant's body, it is necessary to make armatures to support the toy so it will be sturdy enough to stand. Armature wire with a ¼-inch diameter works well, but it is expensive and a wire coat hanger will do as well. First cut off the coat hanger hook (Fig. 7-4a), then straighten the piece of wire. Next cut the wire in half so that there are two pieces, each measuring approximately 16 inches.

Now bend each piece of wire into an arch; then with pliers, bend 1 inch of wire at each end into a loop (Fig. 7-4a). Tape the loops, and any other raw edges, so that they won't puncture the fabric. Insert one of the wire arches into the elephant's back legs and the other arch into the front legs.

The elephant's body is stuffed through the neck opening. First stuff the rear legs *firmly*. Place a pad of stuffing under the loop of each armature end, then stuff around the armatures, so that when you finish you won't be able to feel the armature through the fabric. Next, stuff the body cavity above the rear legs and the center body cavity up to the front legs. Stuff the front legs, padding, and stuffing around the armature as you did the rear legs. Stuff the area above the front legs and the neck.

Use a circular piece of scrap fabric with a diameter ½ inch larger than the neck opening. Turn ¼ inch of fabric to the inside, around the neck edge. Stitch the circle of fabric over the neck opening, turning ¼ inch of fabric to the inside around the edge of the circle as you proceed. This circle of fabric prevents the stuffing from escaping later when you are attaching the head.

Stuff the elephant's head, taking particular care to stuff the trunk so that it is smooth and not lumpy. When you are finished stuffing, cut a circle of scrap fabric about ½ inch larger than the neck opening, and stitch it over the opening in the same manner you stitched the fabric over the body opening.

STEP FIVE

To stitch Elmo's head to his body, first position the head so that the circles that are stitched over the openings are concealed. Then begin your stitching at the center back of the neck. Use an overcast stitch; and with close stitches of equal depth, stitch the two edges firmly together. Stitch around the neck edge twice to ensure that the head is firmly attached.

Insert a plastic ear into each of the cloth ear assemblies. Bend the plastic to fit into the opening, then flatten it out once it is inside the ear. Turn ¼ inch of fabric to the inside around each ear opening. Stitch the opening shut. Stitch an ear to each side of the elephant's head, positioning them along the dotted lines marked on the head fabric.

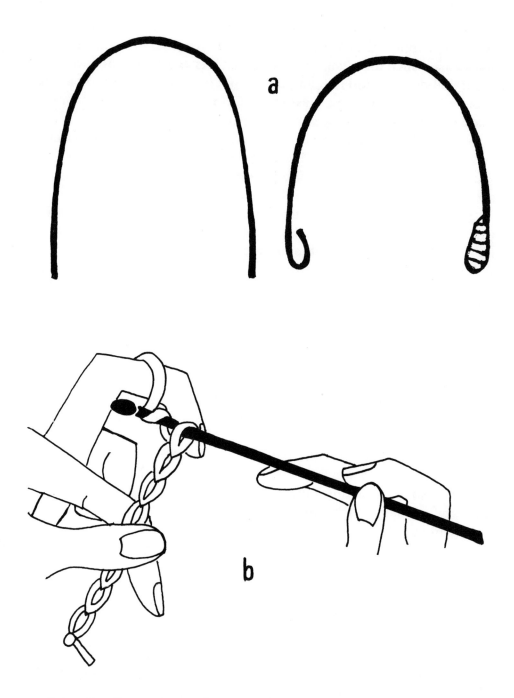

7-4a.   Bending a wire coat hanger into an armature
   b.   Crocheting a chain

STEP SIX

The final step requires some elementary crocheting; a 4-inch chain for Elmo's tail and a 12-inch chain to tie around the neck. (You can substitute ½-inch wide satin ribbon for the neck chain; its purpose, aside from decoration, is to hide the stitching between head and body.) To make a chain, begin with a slip loop (Fig. 7-4b). Hold the loop in your left hand between the thumb and forefinger. Keep the yarn taut over the second and third fingers. Place the crocheting hook through the loop formed by the slip knot. Pass the hook under the yarn on your second and third fingers and draw it through the loop. Continue in this manner until you have a chain of the proper length. Make a 12-inch chain and a 4-inch chain.

Make a pompom by wrapping rug yarn around a 2-inch wide piece of cardboard (Fig. 5-5), approximately 15 times; then remove the yarn and tie it. Clip the ends of the tied piece and fluff out the yarn. Now attach the 4-inch chain with a small piece of yarn to the center of the pompom. Stitch the opposite end of the chain to the elephant's rump with clear nylon thread.

Glue the felt eyes to each side of Elmo's head at the points marked X. Glue the eyelashes under the upper edge of the eyes and the pupils to the eyes. Stitch the eye, the pupil, and the lash to the head with clear nylon thread. Using white acrylic, paint a dot in the center of each eye for a highlight or glue a small piece of white felt if you prefer.

Elmo Elephant is ready to trek through the jungle.

Chapter 8

Sir Charles Camel

> The Arab tugged and pulled as he tightened the ropes which held the heavy bales and boxes to the kneeling camel's back. Then, as the camel arose, his master said jokingly: "What is your preference, camel, the road that goes up hill or the road that goes down?"
>
> "Pray, master," said the camel dryly, "since you leave the choice to me, I would prefer the road that runs along the level plain."
>
> *The Arab and the Camel*
> Aesop

I SAW my first camel in the Central Park Zoo in New York City; it was a young female camel with a blonde, woolly coat. I remember being fascinated by the fact that she walked more like a cat than, as I expected, a horse or a cow; she moved about her pen with a graceful, rhythmic saunter. I have since read that a camel's foot has a re-silient rubbery cushion so that it can walk easily over sand and rough ground. This might explain why camels don't walk like hooved animals.

Like Elmo Elephant, Sir Charles looks particularly nice if made out of sturdy, cotton fabric. A sturdy cotton holds its shape when stuffed; it does not stretch or pull out at the seams, as a lighter fabric might. Decorator cottons take a great deal of wear and tear, but they are expensive; and it may take some searching to find bright and happy prints.

To make an attractive camel, choose a print with desert overtones, that is, prints with yellow, orange, and brown. Choose a stomach fabric of bright orange or yellow taffeta, or satin, to accent the print colors. Sir Charles' tail and harness are rug yarn, the soles of his feet, and his eyes are felt. When completed he measures 16 inches.

8-1   Sir Charles Camel

MATERIALS

½ yard of sturdy cotton print, such as cotton duck, for the body, strip, gusset, and ears.

⅓ yard of taffeta or satin for the belly and the inner ears.

¾ yard of white cotton flannel to line the toy.

9 × 12-inch rectangle of black felt for the soles of the feet and the pupils. A scrap of green or blue felt for the eyes.

A clean, empty plastic bottle to cut up and use for the supports of the soles.

A wire clothes hanger to cut and bend into supports for the legs.

Thread to match the fabric and clear nylon thread.

Kapok or Dacron to stuff the toy.

STEP ONE

Enlarge the patterns for the camel (Figs. 8-2 and 8-3). From the fabrics you have chosen, cut the appropriate number of pieces as marked on the pattern. Transfer the circles for placement of the eyes and the dotted lines for the ears to the *right* side of the two head pieces. Transfer all other markings to the *wrong* side of the fabric.

Cut lining pieces from the cotton flannel for the body, strip, gusset, belly, and ear pieces; and pin them to the *wrong* side of each corresponding piece.

Cut four soles from the plastic bottle. Trim ¼ inch of plastic from the perimeter of each sole. Use the ear pattern and cut two ears from the plastic bottle. Trim ⅜ inch from the perimeter of each ear support and cut ½ inch from each base.

STEP TWO

Note: ¼-inch seams allowed. Unless otherwise stated, stitch fabric with *right* sides together. Remove all pins before turning pieces right side out.

Sir Charles Camel has a graceful body with a lot of curves. In order to properly stuff these curves, it is necessary to leave two openings for stuffing purposes rather than one. As you sew the body together, leave an opening between the two dots marked on the camel's neck and an opening between the two X's marked on his belly.

Begin to assemble Sir Charles by first stiching together the long straight edge of the two belly pieces. Leave an opening between the two

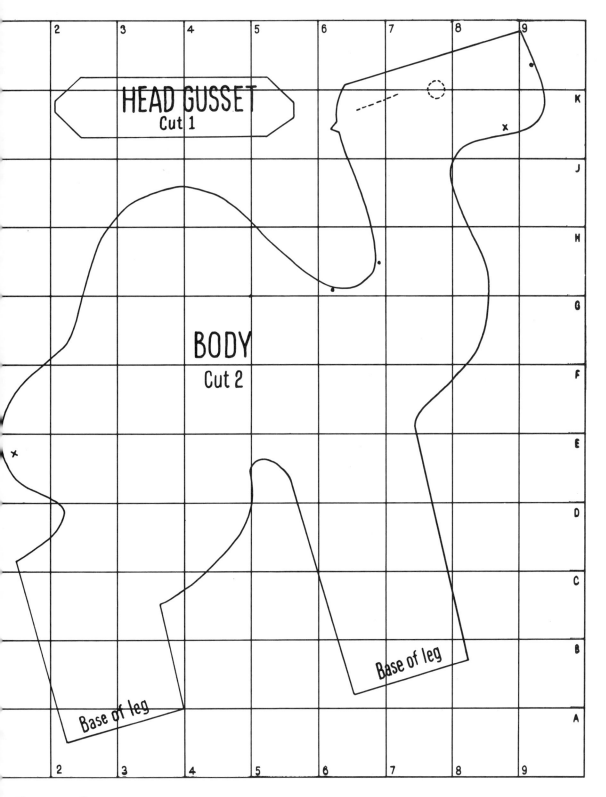

First part of pattern

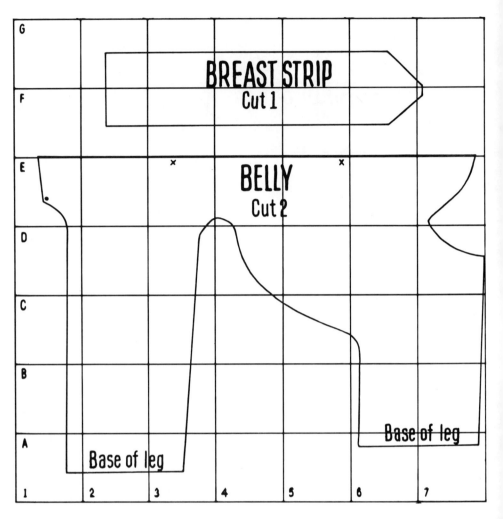

8-3   Second part of pattern

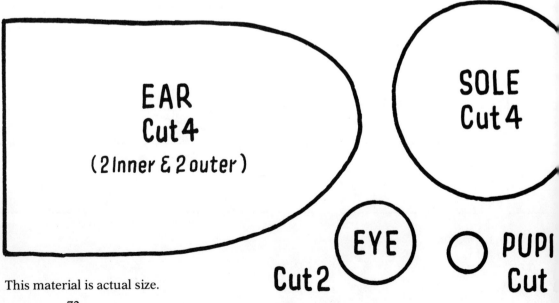

This material is actual size.

X's marked on the fabric. Press the assembled piece flat. Stitch the breast strip between the two dots marked on the belly piece (Fig. 6-3).

Align the front and rear legs of *one* body piece with one *set* of front and rear legs of the belly piece (Fig. 6-4). Pin or baste the two pieces together from the point marked X above the rear hind legs to the point where the breast strip is attached to the belly. Leave the base of the legs open. Now stitch the two pieces together. Repeat the same procedure for the second set of legs.

By hand, baste the breast strip to both sides of the camel's neck from the point where the strip joins the belly piece to the X beneath the chin. Pin the two head pieces together, then baste them to ensure that they remain even. Ease the breast strip to fit the curves of the neck. Stitch the breast strip to the neck. Trim the seams.

With the head still pinned together, stitch from the X marked where the point of the strip is attached beneath the chin to the dot marked on the camel's nose (Fig. 8-4a).

Next, stitch the body pieces together from the X above the rear hind legs to the dot for the neck opening (Fig. 8-4a). Begin stitching again at the second dot and continue stitching to the notch at the base of the head.

Baste the head gusset to both sides of the head, with one tip of the gusset at the notch marked on the base of the head and the second tip at the dot marked on the nose (Fig. 8-4a). Ease the gusset to fit the contours of the head. Stitch the gusset to the head. Trim the seams. Turn the camel right side out through the opening in the belly piece.

Stitch one cotton *outer* ear to one taffeta *inner* ear, leaving the base end open. Stitch the second *outer* ear to the second *inner* ear, leaving the base end open. Turn both ears right side out and press.

STEP THREE

Step three involves sewing a felt sole and plastic inner sole to the bottom of each leg (Fig. 6-6a). To begin, turn ½ inch of fabric inside the base of each leg. Insert a plastic sole into the leg opening so that it forms a flat surface. Cover the plastic sole with a felt sole. If the pieces do not match correctly, trim them to fit.

Stitch the felt to the leg fabric with an overcast stitch. Use clear nylon thread. Stitch around the perimeter of the sole twice. Repeat the procedures above for the remaining three legs.

STEP FOUR

To assure that Sir Charles stands firmly, it is necessary to support him with armatures. Take a wire coat hanger and, with wire cutters, clip off the

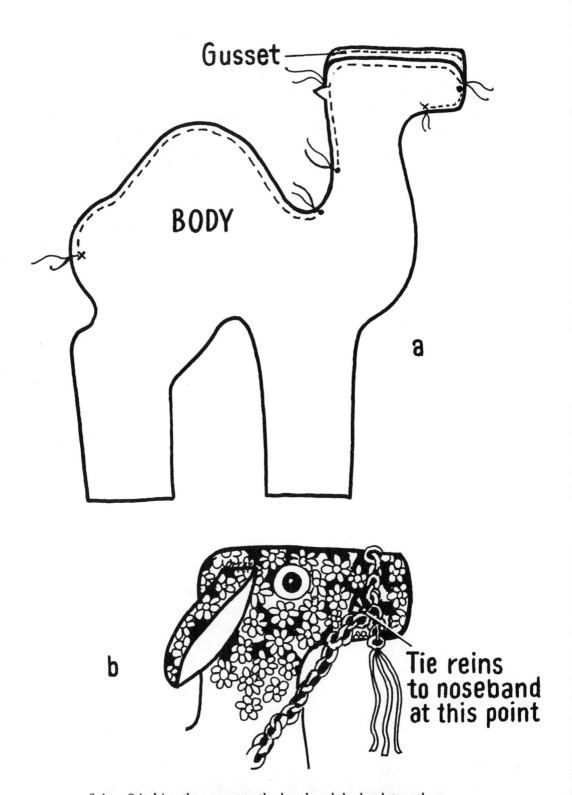

8-4a. Stitching the gusset to the head and the back together
   b. Attaching the harness to the head

hook. Bend the wire into one straight piece. Cut this piece into two equal lengths, each measuring approximately 16 inches. Bend each length into an arch (Fig. 7-4a). With pliers, bend 1 inch at the ends of each arch to form a loop. Wrap the loops with cloth tape, or stuffing, so that no rough wire is left exposed to puncture the fabric. Insert one finished arch through the belly opening and place a taped loop in each rear leg. Now insert the second arch through the opening and place a loop in each of the front legs.

The camel is now ready to be stuffed. Begin with his head and neck. Stuff the animal *firmly*, but do not pack so much stuffing into the doll that it strains the seams. Next stuff the hind legs, padding the armature loops so they cannot easily be felt from the outside. Stuff the camel's thighs and rump, then the front legs, once again padding the armature wire. Now stuff the hump and the center body cavity. Because of the neck curve, the fabric folds and sags in that area. To remedy this, stuff the hollow area of the neck through the neck opening. Use small amounts of stuffing and press it into the neck until the wrinkles in the fabric disappear.

Turn the camel upside down and hold it for support between your knees. Turn ¼ inch of fabric to the inside, around the edges of the belly opening. Use clear nylon thread and stitch this opening tightly and securely closed. Turn the camel right side up. Turn ¼ inch of fabric to the inside, along the edges of the neck opening. Stitch this opening securely closed.

STEP FIVE

Turn ½ inch of fabric to the inside around the base of each of the camel's ears. Insert a plastic ear between the lining fabric of each ear. If the plastic extends beyond the fabric, trim the piece so that it is ¼ inch inside the ear. Turn ¼ inch of fabric around the base of each ear to the inside. Pinch the ear closed, and stitch the pinch together (Fig. 6-6b). Stitch an ear to each side of the camel's head. The ears should be at a right angle to the head and stitched along the dotted line marked on the right side of the head fabric. Securely stitch the ears to the head with nylon thread: ears are vulnerable points on stuffed toys, for young children inevitably tow them around by the ears or the tail.

Sir Charles has a 3½-inch crocheted tail. Crochet a chain of rug yarn to a length of 3½ inches (Fig. 7-4b).

Make a pompom by wrapping yarn around a 2-inch wide piece of cardboard with about 15 turns (Fig. 5-5). Remove the yarn from the cardboard and tie it in the center with a short piece of yarn. Clip the ends of the tied piece and fluff out the yarn. Attach the pompom to the end of the chain by tying the two pieces together with a third piece of yarn. Stitch the opposite end of the chain, *without* the pompom, securely to the camel's rump.

Glue the black felt pupils to the centers of the felt eyes. Glue an eye over each circle marked on the sides of the head. With clear nylon thread stitch the pupil to the eye and the eye to the head. Paint a dab of white acrylic in the center of each pupil for a highlight, or glue and stitch on a small piece of white felt to each pupil for the same effect.

Crochet a 7½-inch chain of rug yarn, leaving a 2-inch piece of un-chained yarn at each end of the chain. Tie this piece of yarn around the camel's nose, with the knot beneath his chin. Unravel the pieces of yarn which hang beneath his chin for a decorative effect. Next chain a 22-inch length of rug yarn for the reins. Thread a large-eyed, sharp needle with a short piece of rug yarn. Stitch this piece of yarn through the nose band, and through the head fabric, about halfway down the side of the head (Fig. 8-4b). Stitch this same piece of yarn through the last loop of the rein. Tie the yarn securely in a knot and trim. Stitch the other end of the rein to the opposite side of the head and noseband.

Last of all, with the large-eyed, sharp needle, stitch five pieces of 2-inch lengths of rug yarn in a row along the top ridge of Sir Charles' hump. Attach each piece so that an equal length of yarn is on each side of the hump. Tie the yarn in a knot. Unravel the pieces to give the illusion of a tuft of fur growing from the hump.

Sir Charles Camel is all set for a journey across the mysterious deserts of a child's imagination.

Chapter 9

Horatio Horse

Ride a cock-horse to Banbury Cross,
To see a fine lady upon a white horse;
Rings on her fingers and bells on her toes,
And she shall have music wherever she goes.

Ride a Cock-Horse
Traditional Nursery Rhyme

*T*HE horse is a romantic animal, associated with the legends of knighthood and chivalry and the fantastic cowboy and Indian adventures of the Old West. Although it would seem logical to assume, in this age of the automobile and the jet plane, that the horse is as much a relic of the past as the paddlewheel boat, this is not the case. In fact, the horse population is increasing each year. More than ever people are riding for leisure and exercise. Then too, unlike motorcycles and automobiles, the horse eats hay, fertilizes the land, and does not pollute the atmosphere.

However, if you are not ready to stable a horse, perhaps Horatio Horse will serve as a temporary substitute. Horatio is a pinto, but he can easily be a bay, or a white horse, or any color you have in mind. His body is cut from ribless or no-wale corduroy, though velvet, velveteen, or brushed denim will work as well. His mane and tail are white rug yarn. The markings and stockings are felt appliqués. For a bay horse, use reddish-brown corduroy, black stocking appliqués, and a black mane and tail. For a palomino use golden corduroy, don't apply any appliqués, and add a white mane and tail. Horatio measures 18 inches tall.

9-1 Horatio Horse

MATERIALS

¾ yard of corduroy fabric for the body, belly, gusset, and outer ears.

A scrap of pink fabric for the inner ears.

¾ yard of white cotton flannel to line the toy.

9 × 12-inch rectangle of black felt for the soles of the feet and the pupils of the eyes.

Scraps of felt in colors to use for appliqués, stockings, and markings.

A scrap of brown felt for the eyes.

Several yards of rug yarn for the mane and tail.

A clean, empty plastic bottle to cut into supports for the bottom of the feet and the ears.

A wire coat hanger for leg armatures.

Kapok or Dacron to stuff the horse.

Thread to match the fabric and clear nylon thread.

STEP ONE

Enlarge the patterns for Horatio Horse (Figs. 9-2 and 9-3). From the fabric you have chosen, cut the appropriate number of pieces as marked on the pattern. Transfer the circles for the eyes and the X's for the ears to the *right* side of the head fabric. Transfer all other markings to the *wrong* side of the fabric.

Now cut duplicates of each piece for lining, except for the eyes and the soles of the feet, and pin them to the *wrong* side of each corresponding piece.

Use the sole pattern as a guide and cut four soles from the plastic bottle. Trim ¼ inch from the perimeter of each piece. Use the ear pattern as a guide and cut two ears from the plastic bottle. Trim ⅜ inch from the perimeter of each ear and trim ¼ inch from each base.

STEP TWO

Note: ¼-inch seams allowed. Unless otherwise stated, stitch fabric with *right* sides together. Remove all pins before turning the assembled piece right side out.

Begin to assemble Horatio Horse by stitching the long, straight edge of the two belly pieces together. Leave an opening between the dots marked on the fabric. Press this piece flat.

Align *one set* of front and rear legs of the belly piece with the front and rear legs of one body piece. Baste the belly to the body from the point marked X above the rear hind legs to the base of the rear hind leg. Leave

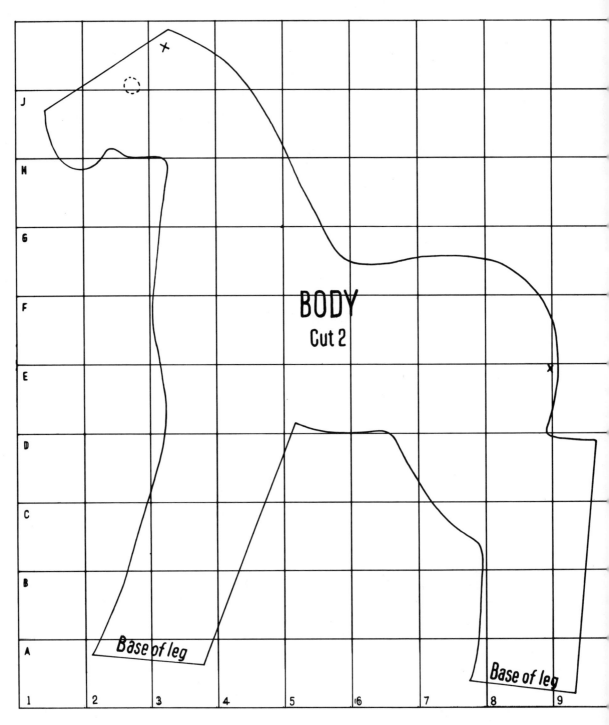

BODY
Cut 2

Base of leg

Base of leg

9-2 First part of pattern

PUPIL
Cut 2

EYE
Cut 2

EAR
Cut 4
(2 Inner & 2 outer)

This material is actual size.

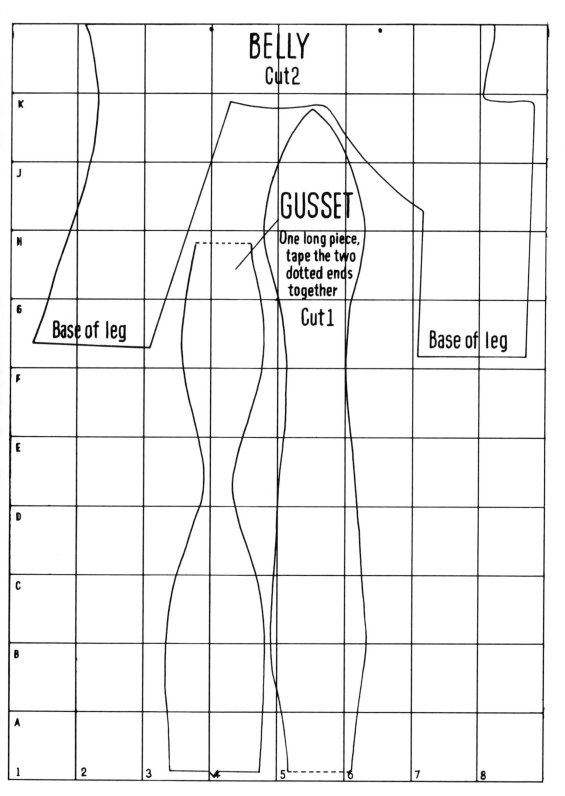

BELLY
Cut 2

GUSSET

One long piece,
tape the two
dotted ends
together

Cut 1

Base of leg

Base of leg

9-3   Second part of pattern

the base of the leg open. Baste together the inside of the rear hind leg, the curve of the belly, and the inside of the front leg to the base of the leg (Fig. 7-3a). Follow along the lines of basting and stitch the belly to the body. Baste and stitch the second side of the belly to the remaining body piece.

Next the gusset is attached. It is one long piece that extends from above the rear hind legs, across the back, over the neck and head and is attached at the base of the chest. Carefully examine Fig. 9-4 before you begin to stitch. The pointed end of the gusset fits in the V formed above the rear hind legs, where the two body pieces are attached at the place marked X. Baste one side of the pointed gusset tip to one edge of the V of the body piece and continue to baste the gusset along the back, easing the gusset to fit the curves, then along the neck, around the head, under the chin, and finally down the chest. Leave ½ inch at the base of the gusset unattached. Now baste the other side of the gusset to the second body

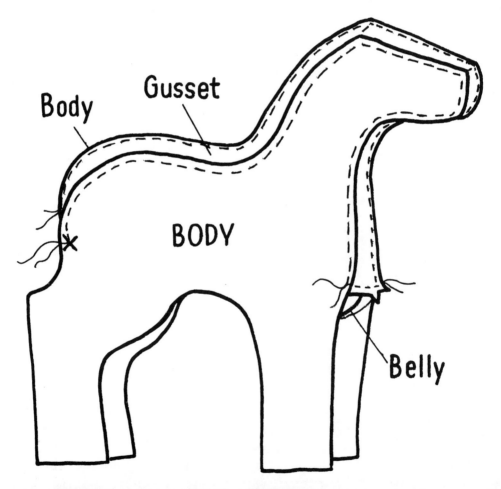

9-4   Stitching the gusset to the body of the horse

piece. Machine stitch each side of the gusset to the body pieces. Next, stitch the notched edge of the gusset to the belly piece, attaching it between the two dots marked on the belly piece.

Stitch the front seam of the front legs, beginning at the base of each leg and stitching to the point where belly, gusset, and body piece join.

Trim the seams and remove any pins. Turn the horse right side out through the belly opening.

Stitch one inner ear to one outer ear, leaving the base open. Assemble the second ear. Turn the ears right side out and press.

STEP THREE

Each of Horatio's legs is open at the base. To give his legs a natural cylindrical appearance, it is necessary to sew a felt sole and a plastic sole support to the base of each leg. Refer to Fig. 6-6a before proceeding. Turn ½ inch of fabric to the inside, around the base of one leg. Insert a plastic sole into the opening so that it forms a flat surface. Place a felt sole over the plastic. If either the plastic or felt sole does not fit the opening correctly, trim the piece. Overcast the felt sole to the base of the leg, using stitches which are short, close together, and of equal depth. Because the soles need to be durable (children have a tendency to ride the horses), use clear nylon thread. Now sew a felt sole with a plastic insert to the base of the other legs.

STEP FOUR

To make the armatures for Horatio's legs, take a wire coat hanger; and with wire cutters, clip off the hook. Bend the remaining wire into one straight piece. Cut this piece into two equal lengths, approximately 16 inches each. Bend each length into an arch (Fig. 7-4a). With pliers, bend the ends of each arch to form a 1-inch loop. Wrap the loops with cloth tape so that no rough wire is left exposed to puncture the fabric. Fit an arch through the belly opening and insert one loop into each hind leg. Insert the second arch into the front legs.

Horatio should be stuffed *firmly*. Use small wads of stuffing packed closely together. Stuffing settles and if there are gaps, the horse will droop.

First stuff the head, filling out the cavity firmly. Next, stuff the neck, then switch to the rear legs and place a pad of stuffing under each armature loop. Stuff the legs, taking care to conceal the wire by stuffing all around it. Stuff the front legs in the same manner. Stuff the chest, working from the neck down. This is a touchy area. Be sure to pack the stuffing around and under the curve of the armature wire. When finished with the chest, stuff the rump. Lastly, stuff the center body cavity. The horse should have a sleek appearance and be firm to the touch. Run your fingers over Horatio's body. If you detect any gaps or hollows in the stuffing, fill them.

Turn ¼ inch of fabric to the inside, along the length of the belly opening. Stitch the opening securely closed with clear nylon thread.

If bits of stuffing are clinging to the surface of the horse, brush them off with a lint brush.

STEP FIVE

Now that the body is finished, it's time to add the finishing touches. The color and the placement of the ears, eyes, markings, tail, and mane will give Horatio his character.

Begin by turning ½ inch of fabric to the inside, around the base of each ear. Insert a plastic ear between the lining fabric of each ear. If necessary, trim the plastic for a correct fit. Stitch the base of each ear closed. Pinch the base of the ear together and stitch the pinch closed (Fig. 6-6b). Stitch an ear securely to each side of Horatio's head at the points marked X.

Glue black felt pupils to the brown eyes. Glue the eyes to the circles marked with dotted lines on each side of the head. After the glue has dried, stitch the felt to the fabric. Paint a dab of white acrylic paint in the center of each eye for a highlight or cut small pieces of white felt then glue and stitch them to the pupils.

To determine shape and size of the appliqués you will use for markings, first make a full-sized sketch of the horse, then draw the kind of markings you would like him to have. Cut pieces of felt to match the shape and size of these markings. Try the felt markings on the horse to be sure they look right. If not, shift them around a bit. When you are satisfied with the arrangement, glue the felt to the body fabric with nontoxic cloth glue. When the glue is dry, stitch the edges of the felt markings to the fabric.

To make Horatio's tail, cut ten lengths of rug yarn, each 12 inches long. Thread a piece of yarn through a large-eyed, sharp needle. Stitch the yarn through the fabric at the point on the rump where you want the tail. Pull the yarn through the fabric until there is an *equal* length on each side of the point where the needle penetrated the fabric (Fig. 9-5b). Tie the two ends of the yarn in a knot. Stitch the remaining nine pieces of yarn to the rump, grouping them as close together as possible. Unravel each strand of yarn for.a curly effect.

To make Horatio's mane, you will need to cut thirty-four lengths of rug yarn, each 12 inches. Look at Fig. 9-5a, then, with the large-eyed, sharp needle, stitch four lengths of yarn in a row between the ears, again pulling the yarn halfway through the fabric, then knotting it as you did for the tail.

Kronkite Clown, the Owl and the Pussy-cat, and Timothy Dragon

Sister Pat, Tallulah Ballerina, and Brother Philly

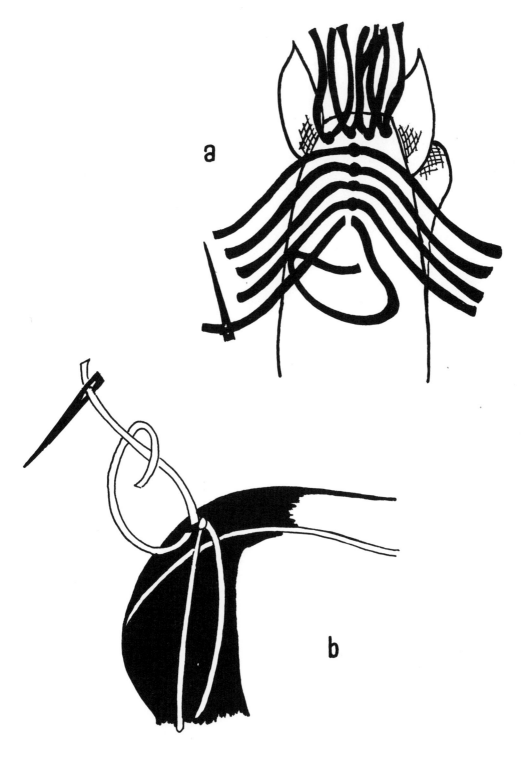

9-5a. Stitching the mane to the neck of the horse
   b. Stitching the tail to the rump of the horse

These four lengths of yarn will fall forward over the face, to represent Horatio's forelock. Next, stitch the remaining thirty lengths of rug yarn close together in a row, down the center of the neck, then unravel them. As the mane of a horse always seems to fall to the same side, brush the yarn to one side or the other. Trim the mane.

Horatio is now finished, and ready for a good gallop, unless of course you would like to crochet him a halter or bridle. If you are really ambitious, you can make him a felt saddle, a blanket, and a nosebag. Also keep in mind that horses are herd animals and get lonely without company.

Chapter 10

The Three Bears

Once upon a time there were three
Bears and they lived in the woods in
their own house. One was a wee tiny
Bear; and one was an inbetween,
middle-sized Bear; and one was a very
large-sized Bear.

The Three Bears
Traditional Folk Tale

*T*HE first "teddy" bear was presented to the toy market in 1903 by Morris Michtom, founder of the Ideal Toy Corporation. Michtom got the idea from a political cartoon that appeared in the *Washington Post,* drawn by Clifford Berryman, showing Teddy Roosevelt refusing to shoot a bear cub that had crossed his path on a hunting expedition in the Rocky Mountains; an incident that actually occurred. The teddy bear has been a fantastic and lasting success. Children and adults have made stuffed bears confidants and companions ever since.

Mama, Poppa, and Baby Bear are cut from pile fabric, but velvet, velveteen, imitation fur, or real fur can be substituted: an old fur coat would make a particularly nice bear. I've made each member of the Bear family two different colors. Poppa is blue and white; Mama is brown and orange; Baby is yellow and orange. Colored buttons are used for the eyes and nose. Again, different colors help give each bear its own personality. You can make all three bears, or one or two. Poppa Bear measures 23 inches tall; Mama Bear measures 19 inches; Baby Bear 12 inches.

10-1   The Three Bears

MATERIALS

Poppa Bear ½ yard of pile fabric for the back, head, legs, arms, tail, and ears.

¼ yard of pile fabric in another color for the gusset, stomach, base, soles of the feet, and paw patches.

A scrap of pink fabric for the inner ears, and scraps of felt for the eye patches.

Two matching buttons for the eyes, and a flat, shiny black button for the nose.

1 yard of ribbon 1-inch wide to tie in a neck bow.

Kapok or Dacron to stuff the doll.

Thread to match the fabric and clear nylon thread.

Mama Bear ½ yard of pile fabric for the back, head, legs, arms, tail, and ears.

¼ yard of pile fabric in another color for the gusset, stomach, base, soles of the feet, and paw patches.

A scrap of pink fabric for the inner ears, and scraps of felt for the eye patches.

Two matching buttons for the eyes, and a flat, shiny button for a nose.

¾ yard of ribbon 1-inch wide to tie in a bow around her neck, and 1 yard of ribbon 1-inch wide in another color for her apron waistband.

A 12-inch square piece of fabric for the apron.

A 15-inch length of lace edging 1-inch wide to trim the apron.

Kapok or Dacron to stuff the doll.

Thread to match the fabric and clear nylon thread.

Baby Bear ¼ yard of pile fabric for the back, head, legs, arms, tail, and ears.

⅛ yard of pile fabric in another color for the gusset, stomach, base, soles of the feet, and paw patches.

A scrap of pink fabric for the inner ears, and scraps of felt for the eye patches.

Two matching buttons for the eyes, and a flat, shiny button for a nose.

½ yard of ribbon ½-inch wide to tie in a bow around his neck.

A 7-inch square of white felt for the diaper.

Kapok or Dacron to stuff the doll.

Thread to match the fabric and clear nylon thread.

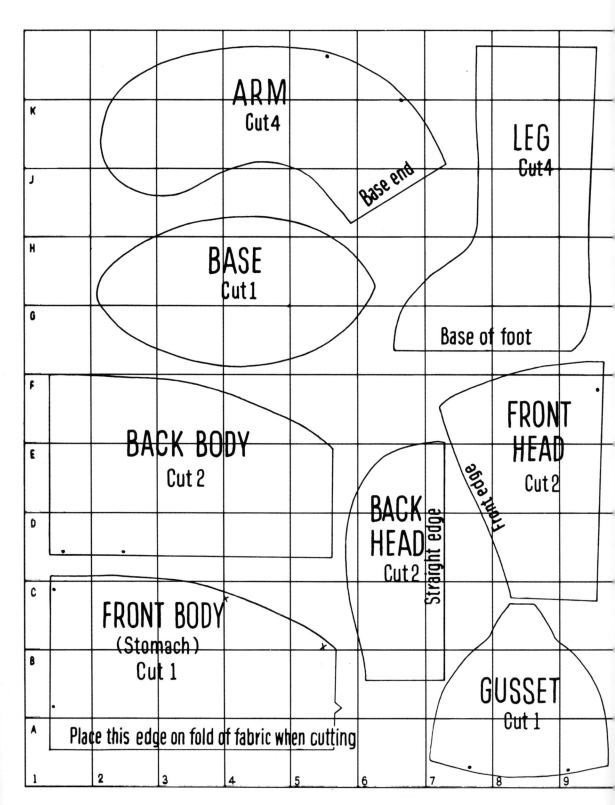

ARM
Cut 4

LEG
Cut 4

Base end

BASE
Cut 1

Base of foot

BACK BODY
Cut 2

FRONT
HEAD
Cut 2

Front edge

BACK
HEAD
Cut 2

Straight edge

FRONT BODY
(Stomach)
Cut 1

GUSSET
Cut 1

Place this edge on fold of fabric when cutting

K J H G F E D C B A

1 2 3 4 5 6 7 8 9

10-2   Poppa Bear

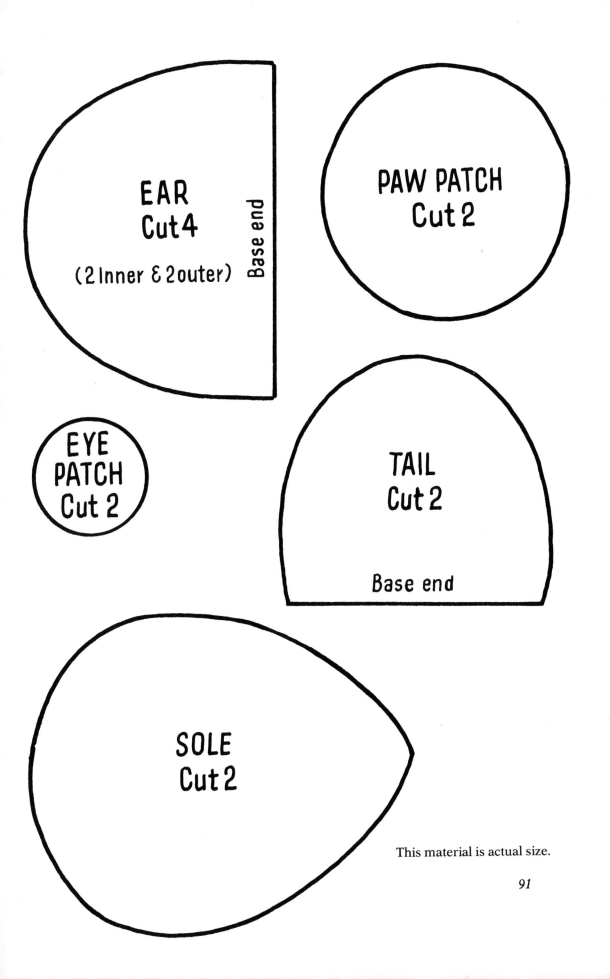

EAR
Cut 4

(2 Inner & 2 outer)

Base end

PAW PATCH
Cut 2

EYE
PATCH
Cut 2

TAIL
Cut 2

Base end

SOLE
Cut 2

This material is actual size.

91

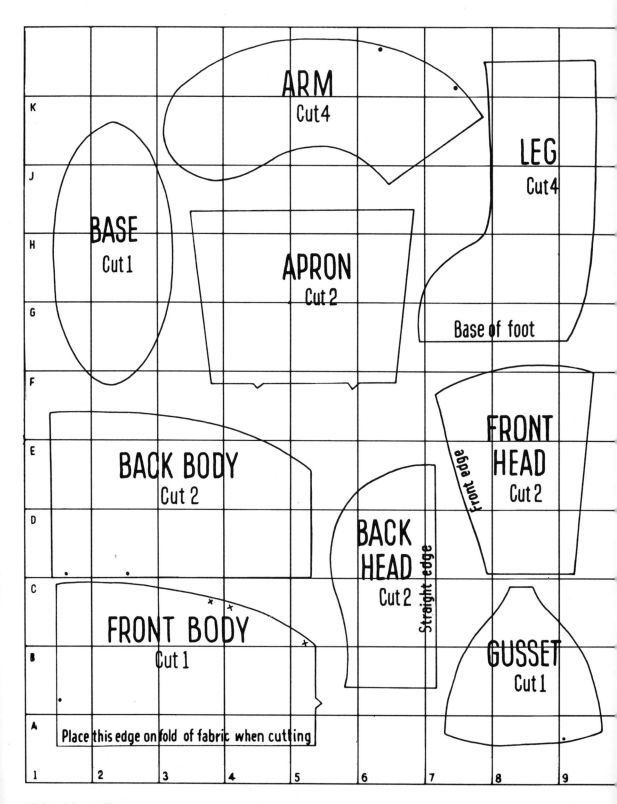

ARM
Cut 4

LEG
Cut 4

BASE
Cut 1

APRON
Cut 2

Base of foot

BACK BODY
Cut 2

FRONT
HEAD
Cut 2

Front edge

BACK
HEAD
Cut 2

Straight edge

FRONT BODY
Cut 1

GUSSET
Cut 1

Place this edge on fold of fabric when cutting

10-3   Mama Bear

92

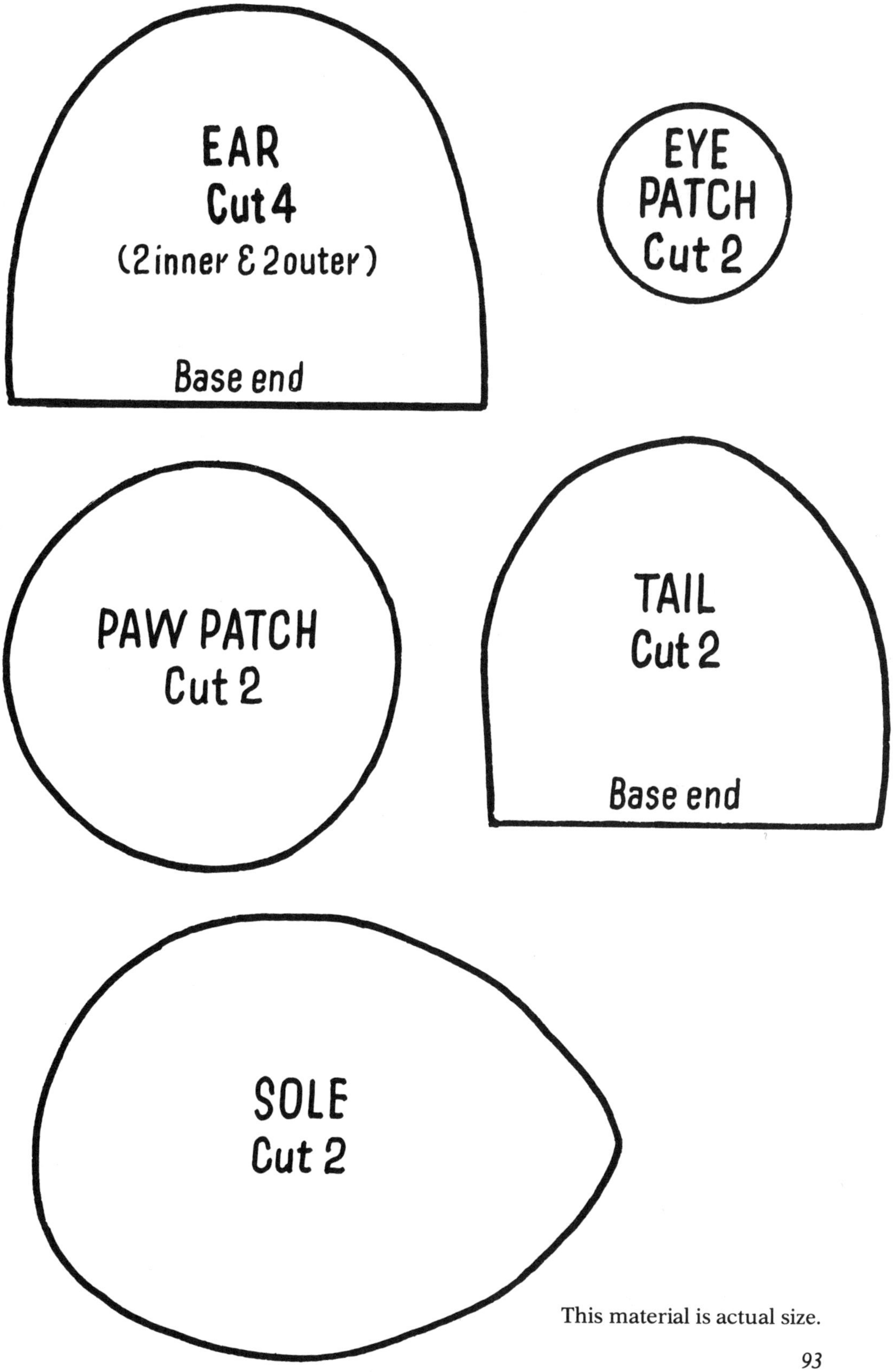

EAR
Cut 4
(2 inner & 2 outer)

Base end

EYE PATCH
Cut 2

PAW PATCH
Cut 2

TAIL
Cut 2

Base end

SOLE
Cut 2

This material is actual size.

93

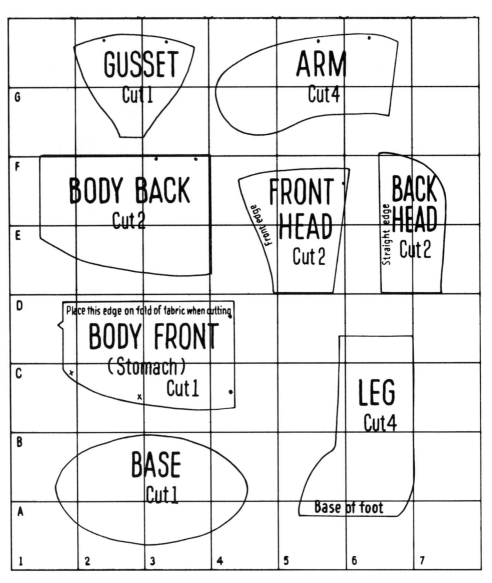

10-4   Baby Bear

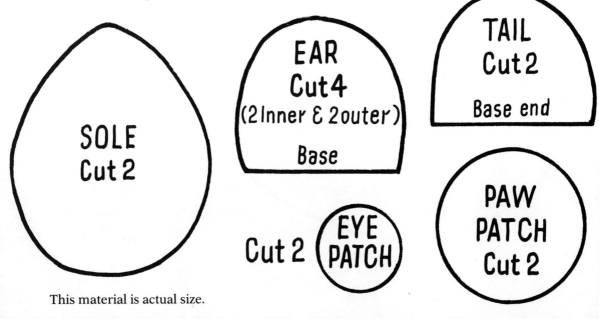

This material is actual size.

STEP ONE

Enlarge the patterns for the three Bears (Figs. 10-2, 10-3, and 10-4). From the fabrics you have chosen, cut the appropriate number of pieces, as marked on the pattern. Cut the pieces for the back, head, legs, arms, ears, and tail from one color of pile fabric. Cut the pieces for the stomach, gusset, base, soles of the feet, and paw patches from another color pile fabric. Cut the inner ears from pink fabric and the eye patches from felt. Transfer all markings to the *wrong* side of the fabric.

STEP TWO

> *Note:* ¼-inch seams allowed. Stitch with *right* sides together unless otherwise stated. Remove all pins before turning the assembled pieces right side out.

Each bear's head is a single assembly. The body, arms, and legs are stitched together to make up a second piece. Each of the two assembled pieces is stuffed separately and then they are sewn together. The following instructions apply to each of the three Bears.

First the head is assembled. Stitch the *straight* edge of the two *back* head pieces together (Fig. 10-5a). Stitch the *front* edge of the two *front* head pieces together. Baste the gusset between the two front head pieces. The three pieces should come together at the nose (Fig. 10-5b). Stitch the pieces together.

Stitch a pink *inner* ear to each *outer* ear. Leave the base of the ears unstitched. Turn the ear right side out. Make a topstitch ¼ inch from the outer edge around the perimeter of each ear and leave the base open. Do the same for the other ear.

Pin an ear between each set of dots marked on the *front* head piece (Fig. 10-5c). Make sure the *pink* side of the ear and the *right* side of the fabric are together. The base of the ear should extend ¼ inch beyond the edge of the fabric. Baste the ears in place.

Baste the *curved* edge of the *back* head piece to the *open* edge of the front head piece (Fig. 10-5c). Position the center seam of the *back* piece *midway* between the two seams of the *gusset* (now part of the front head piece). Stitch the front to the back, catching in the ears. Trim the seam. Turn the head right side out.

Stitch the tail pieces together, leaving the base open. Turn the tail right side out, then place a pad of stuffing in it. Pin the tail to the *right* side of one back body piece, between the two dots marked on the fabric. The base of the tail should extend ¼ inch beyond the edge of the fabric. Baste between the dots. Place the second back body piece over the one to which the tail is basted. Stitch the center back seam, catching in the tail.

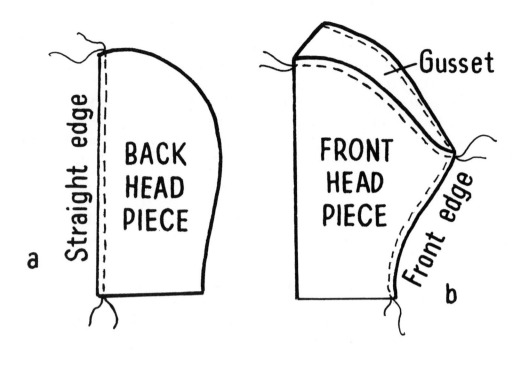

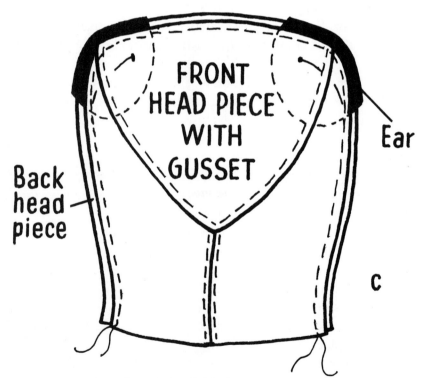

10-5a. Stitching together the back head piece
   b. Stitching together the front pieces and stitching the gusset to the head
   c. Stitching the back head piece to the front head piece, catching in the ears

There are four arm pieces, two for each arm. Stitch each pair together, leaving an opening between the two dots marked on the lower side of each arm and also leaving open the base of each arm. Turn the arms right side out.

There are four leg pieces, two for each leg. Stitch each pair together, leaving *both* ends of the legs open. Turn the pieces right side out.

Pin an arm to each side of the stomach piece, between the X's marked on each side of the fabric (Fig. 10-6). The arms should curve upward toward the neck edge. Baste the arms to the fabric.

Pin a leg between each pair of dots marked on the base of the stomach piece (Fig. 10-6). Be sure that the feet point *inward*, toward the belly,

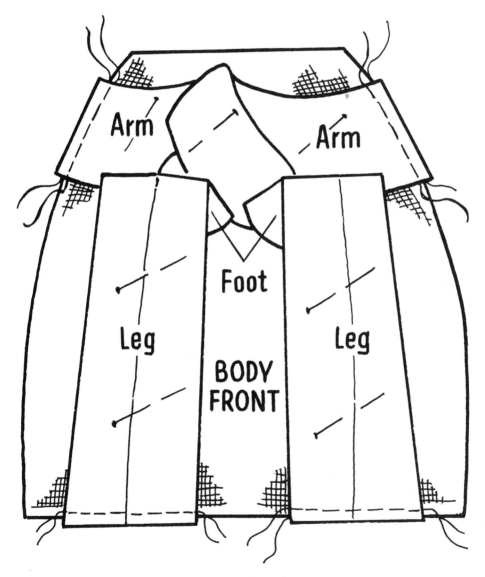

10-6   Basting the arms and legs to the body front

otherwise when you turn the body right side out, the legs will be on backward. Baste the legs to the fabric.

With right side of the fabric together, align the back body piece with the front body piece to which the arms and legs are pinned and basted. Stitch each side seam, catching in the arms. Stitch the shoulder seams, leaving an opening between the notches and an opening at bottom for the base piece.

Attaching the base piece is important. If it is improperly attached, the toy will be lopsided. For this reason, it is a good idea to baste before stitching. First place the base piece over the opening in the base of the toy. Pin it in place. If it overlaps the edges, trim it, taking care to maintain an even curve. Baste the base piece to the toy (Fig. 16-6a). Stitch, catching in the legs which are now attached to the front body piece. Remove all pins. Turn the bear right side out through the neck opening.

STEP THREE

The bears begin to take shape as they are stuffed. I recommend you use Dacron to stuff them, because it is washable, and teddy bears often are long childhood companions and require an occasional washing.

Start with the legs. Turn ¼ inch of fabric to the inside, around the base of one foot. Stitch a sole over the opening; and as you proceed, turn ¼ inch of fabric to the inside, around the edges of the sole. Stop stitching when there is a 1-inch wide opening remaining. Stuff the leg through this opening. Use the blunt end of a pencil to push the stuffing into the thigh. The bear should not be stuffed too firmly; his limbs should be soft and squeezable. When you finish stuffing the leg, continue and sew the opening closed, stitching around the base of the foot a second time. Follow the same procedures to stuff the second leg.

Stuff each arm through the opening in the underside. Stitch the opening closed, turning ¼ inch of fabric along the open edges to the inside.

Stuff the body cavity, but leave enough room so you will be able to insert the neck. Now, stuff the head.

Insert the neck into the body opening. Turn ¼ inch of fabric to the inside, around the neck edge. Stitch the head securely to the neck fabric. Stitch around the neck edge at least twice.

To release any pile caught in the seams, comb gently along the seamline with a fine-toothed comb.

STEP FOUR

This last step involves attaching the features. Position the eye patches on the head, halfway between the ears and the nose, overlapping the gusset seam. Now glue the eye patches to the head; and when the glue dries, stitch the patches to the fabric. Experiment with a variety of buttons, placing them in the center of the eye patches until you find an expression you like. You will be amazed how expressive button eyes can be. Next stitch the buttons to the center of the eye patches.

For a nose, stitch a flat, shiny button to the tip of the gusset.

Stitch a paw patch to the center front of each paw, turning the raw edges of the patch to the inside as you proceed.

Tie a ribbon in a bow around the neck of each bear.

To make Mama Bear's apron, stitch together three sides of the fabric, leaving the notched edge open. Turn the piece right side out, then tuck ¼ inch of fabric along the notched edges to the inside and press the entire piece. Topstitch the lace edging to the three stitched sides.

Next, the ribbon for the waistband has to be stitched to the apron. First find the middle of the ribbon length (measure it with a ruler or fold it in half), then mark this middle point with a dot on the wrong side. Align the dot against the apron, midway between the two notches, with about ¼ inch of ribbon overlapping the apron edge (Fig. 17-4b). Stitch the ribbon to the apron, placing two rows of stitching side by side. The first row of stitching should be ⅛ inch within the apron's edge and the second row should be ¼ inch below the first. These rows will stitch together the notched edge of the apron as well as attach the ribbon. As you stitch, catch in the edges of the lace. When the apron is ready, tie the ribbon around Mama Bear's waist.

Baby Bear wears a diaper. If you use a fabric other than felt, hem the edges. Fold the diaper as you would an actual baby's diaper, but instead of pinning it, stitch the corners together.

The Bear Family is ready for their porridge.

Chapter 11

Cavalier Cat

Pussy cat, pussy cat, where have you been?
I've been to London to look at the Queen.
Pussy cat, pussy cat, what did you there?
I frightened a little mouse under her chair.

Pussy-Cat
Traditional Nursery Rhyme

*T*HERE is an aloofness and a special independence
that cats possess which makes their moments of affection very special. Unlike dogs, who will serve their masters, cats are usually out for themselves, for sustenance and adventure. Dogs are loyal and knight-like in their devotion; cats are more debonair and cavalier in their attitudes.

Cavalier Cat is a dashing, handsome long-haired fellow; and though his days are spent in the search for adventure, he is content to curl up at night in the warm, peaceful presence of a child. He is cut from fake fur fabric—the long shaggy variety. If you plan to make this cat, be on the lookout for fur remnants at your local fabric store, or you may have an out of style fake fur coat that can be cut up. Good quality fake fur wears well, and the shag hides seamlines and topstitching, giving the finished toy a neat professional appearance. Cavalier Cat measures 22 inches.

11-1   Cavalier Cat

MATERIALS

A 24 × 60-inch piece of fake fur, for the body, base, arms, legs, outer ears, and gusset.

A scrap of pink cotton fabric for the inner ears.

A 9 × 12-inch rectangle of bright colored felt for the hat.

Scraps of felt in a variety of colors for the feathers, features, and hatband; and a scrap of pink satin or taffeta for the nose.

A 9 × 12-inch piece of felt for the pocketbook.

A 9 × 12-inch piece of dark felt for the bottoms of the feet.

Two buttons with 1½-inch diameters for the eyes; and two ¼-inch diameter buttons, black with rhinestone centers, for the pupils.

1 yard each of satin ribbon, in two different colors, to tie in a bow around his neck and to use as a sash around his waist.

A clean, empty plastic bottle, to cut up and use as reinforcements for the soles of the feet.

Kapok or Dacron to stuff the toy.

Thread to match the fabric and clear nylon thread.

STEP ONE

Enlarge the patterns for Cavalier Cat (Figs. 11-2 and 11-3). *Tape* the body patterns to the *wrong* side of the fur fabric. Use masking or transparent tape: it is difficult to pin fur fabric. Now, with small, sharp scissors, cut through the backing, trying not to shear the nap. Next cut pieces for the hat, feathers, features, hatband, pocketbook, and soles of the feet from the felt you have chosen. Don't forget to cut the right number of pieces as marked on each pattern. Transfer all markings to the *wrong* side of the fabric.

Using the sole pattern as a guide, cut two reinforcements from the plastic bottle for the soles of the feet. Trim ½ inch from the perimeter of each plastic sole.

STEP TWO

Note: ½-inch seams allowed. Unless otherwise stated, stitch the fabric with *right* sides together. Remove all pins before turning assembled pieces right side out.

Sewing on fake fur can be a trying experience, especially the bulky, long-shagged varieties. Experiment with different machine settings on

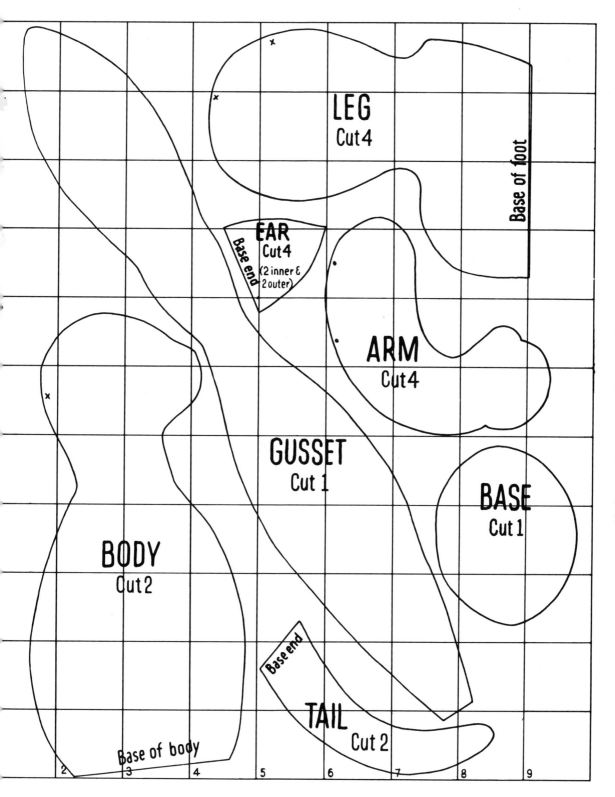

LEG
Cut 4

Base of foot

EAR
Cut 4
(2 inner &
2 outer)

Base end

ARM
Cut 4

GUSSET
Cut 1

BASE
Cut 1

BODY
Cut 2

Base end

TAIL
Cut 2

Base of body

2   7   3   4   5   6   7   8   9

2   First part of pattern

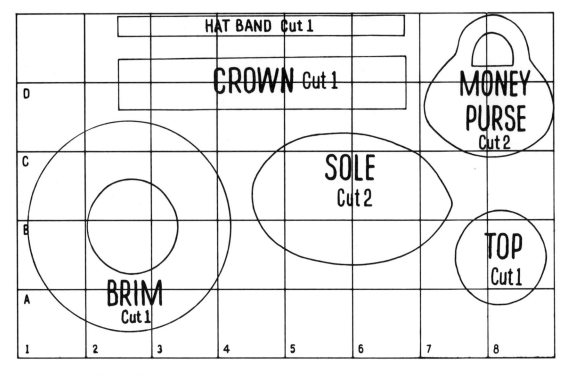

11-3   Second part of pattern

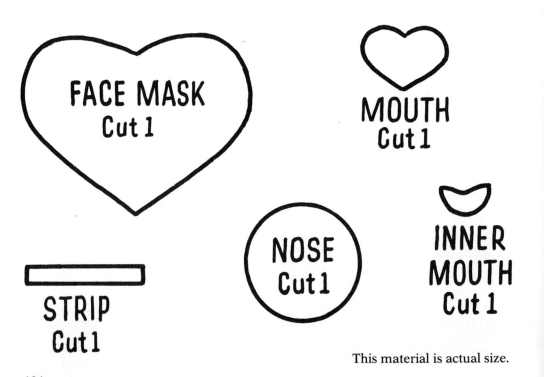

This material is actual size.

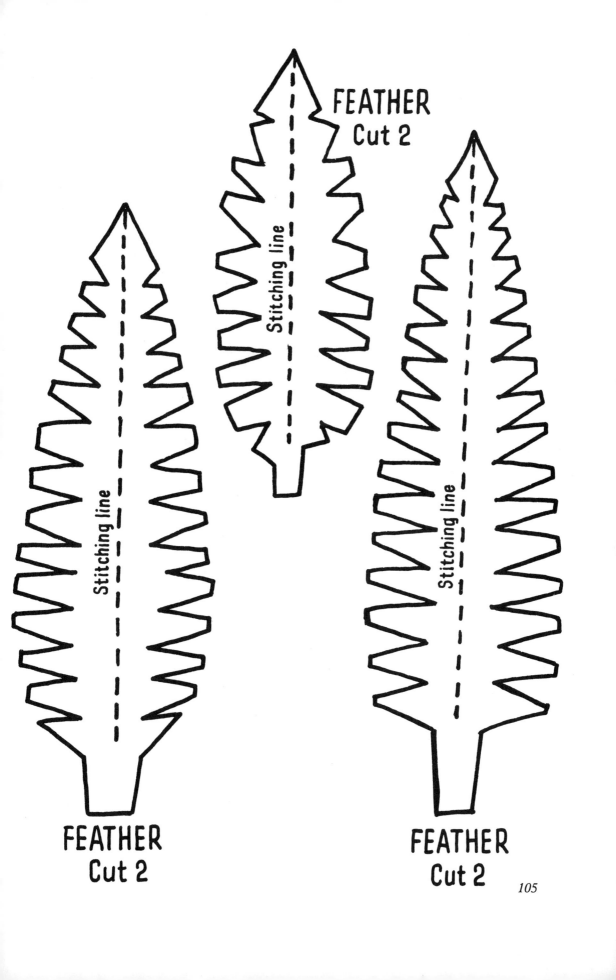

FEATHER
Cut 2

Stitching line

FEATHER
Cut 2

Stitching line

FEATHER
Cut 2

Stitching line

105

scrap fabric. Maximum pressure is usually recommended for heavy fabrics, but I prefer to lower the feed dog and guide the fur through by hand. If you can't adjust your machine to stitch fur properly, don't give up. Stitch the toy together by hand.

Begin Cavalier Cat by stitching the two body pieces together from the base of the back to the X marked at the back of the head. Next, baste the gusset between the two body pieces (Fig. 11-4). The pointed tip of the gusset should fit into the V formed by the two body pieces at the point marked X. Baste one side of the gusset to one body piece, starting at the X and easing the gusset around the head, under the chin, and down the front of the body. Baste the second side of the gusset to the second body piece. Trim the base of the toy even. Stitch the gusset to each body piece. Turn

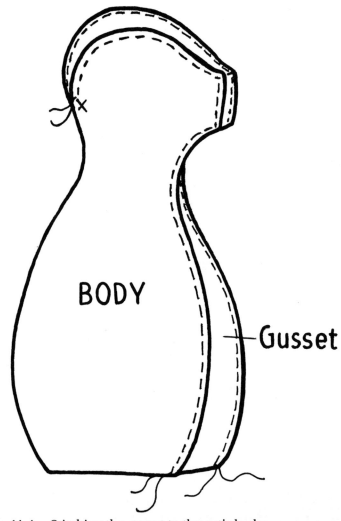

11-4   Stitching the gusset to the cat's body

the body of the toy right side out. Use a comb and carefully pull out any fur caught in the seams.

There are four arm pieces, two for each arm. Stitch each pair together around the entire perimeter, leaving an opening between the dots marked on the underside of each arm. Turn each arm right side out and comb the fur from the seams.

There are four leg pieces, two for each leg. Stitch each pair together. Leave an opening between the two X's marked at each thigh and leave the base of each foot open. Turn the legs right side out and comb the trapped fur from the seams.

Stitch one pink *inner* ear to one fur *outer* ear, leaving the base open. Assemble the second ear. Turn both ears right side out and comb the fur from the seams.

Stitch the two tail pieces together, leaving the base open. Turn the tail right side out and remove any fur from the seams.

STEP THREE

First stuff Cavalier Cat's body, pushing wads of stuffing up into his head, and then stuff the main body cavity. Because fur fabric does not show every little gap in the stuffing as does cotton or other fabrics with short naps, Cavalier Cat does not have to be stuffed as firmly as Horatio Horse. Make him firm, but squeezable.

After you stuff the body, turn ½ inch of fabric to the inside, around the opening in the bottom of the toy. Stitch the base piece over the opening and, as you proceed, turn ½ inch of fabric around the edges of the base to the inside. Double stitch the base for security.

Turn ½ inch of fabric to the inside, around the base of the ears. Stitch the base of the ears closed. Stitch an ear securely to each side of the cat's head, positioning them so that they look natural.

Stuff each arm through the opening in the seam. Turn ½ inch of fabric to the inside, along the edges of the opening. Stitch the opening closed. Stitch an arm to each side of the cat's body at shoulder level. If you have difficulty attaching the arms with a straight needle, try using a curved mattress needle; it is ideally suited for this purpose.

Lightly stuff the tail to within 2 inches of the open end. Turn ½ inch of fabric to the inside, around the edges of the opening. Stitch the opening closed. Stitch the tail to the center of the lower back.

STEP FOUR

Cavalier Cat's feet may seem slightly large in proportion to his body, but it is necessary that they be large so that he can stand firmly. It is also important that his soles be flat and firm and that his ankles and feet be stuffed *firmly*. If the stuffing is not firm here, it will shift, resulting in wobbly legs.

Turn ½ inch of fabric to the inside, around the base of one foot. Insert into the opening one of the plastic soles you cut previously from the plastic bottle. If the plastic does not fit properly, trim it. Lay a felt sole over the plastic sole (Fig. 6-6a), and stitch it to the base of the foot. An overcast stitch works well for this. Keep the stitches close together and of equal depth. Stitch the second sole to the second foot in the same manner.

Firmly stuff the feet and ankles. The thighs should be stuffed slightly less firm than the ankles: it is difficult to attach the legs to the body if the stuffing in the thighs is too firm. Now, turn ½ inch of fabric to the inside, around the edges of the opening in the side of the leg. Stitch each opening shut.

Stitch a thigh to each side of the cat's body. A mattress needle comes in handy here as well. Stand the doll up from time to time as you stitch to make sure that the legs are being attached firmly and evenly so that it will stand properly.

STEP FIVE

Cavalier Cat's face is next. He has button eyes, a satin nose, and a mouth and face mask of felt.

Glue the face mask to the head. The upper edge of the mask should be halfway between the chin and an imaginary axis between the ears. After the glue has dried, stitch the mask to the face. Liquid latex is excellent for gluing fabric together, but there are other glues on the market specifically for cloth.

For the nose, run a basting stitch around the nose fabric (Fig. 11-5b), then place a pad of stuffing about the size of a nickle in the center of the *wrong* side of the piece. Now draw up the stitching by pulling the ends, so that the fabric gathers around and partially covers the stuffing, as indicated. Now place the nose piece, stuffing side down, on the center front of the cat's face, in the V formed by the face mask. Stitch the edges of the nose to the fabric.

Glue the thin felt strip to the face mask vertically, the upper end of the strip just touching the nose. Next glue the mouth onto the face mask, over the lower edge of the felt strip. Glue the inner heart-shaped mouth to the center of the larger mouth piece. The inner mouth piece should be a darker color for contrast: if the larger mouth piece is pink, make it red or black. Now glue three dots of black felt to the face mask on each side of the strip, arranging them so they look like whiskers. When the glue has dried, stitch all the pieces to the face mask.

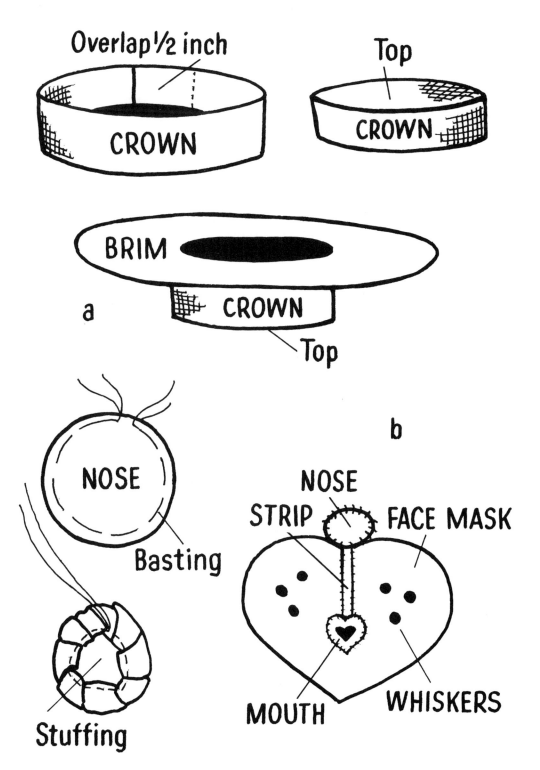

Overlap ½ inch

CROWN

Top

CROWN

BRIM

CROWN

Top

a

b

NOSE

Basting

Stuffing

NOSE

STRIP

FACE MASK

MOUTH

WHISKERS

11-5a.   Assembling the hat
   b.   Basting the nose piece, drawing up the stitching and stitching the nose to
        the head

For eyes, stitch a rhinestone button to the center of each green button, then stitch each button eye to the center of the cat's head, above and a little to the outside of the face mask.

Cavalier Cat's hat is glued together in three steps (Fig. 11-5a). First overlap ½ inch the ends of the strip which will form the crown and glue the ends together. Allow the crown to dry before continuing.

Next place a line of glue around the lower edge of the crown, slip the brim over the crown, then slide it from the top down over the line of glue. Prop this piece upside down and support the brim so it dries without sticking to your table top or work bench.

After the brim has dried, glue the circular piece to the top of the crown by running a line of glue around the edge of the piece and setting it firmly on the crown.

For the hat band, glue the strip of contrasting felt around the crown, joining it at the back of the hat. Fold the brim up and, with a few stitches, attach it to the crown.

Each felt feather has two pieces; there are six pieces altogether. Glue each of the three pairs together. After the glue has dried, run a line of contrasting color stitching down the center of each felt feather; then slip them into the brim fold and stitch them in place.

Tie a ribbon in a bow around Cavalier Cat's neck.

Topstitch together the two pieces of the money purse, stitching ⅛ inch from the outer edge, leaving the inside edge open so a penny or two can be slipped into the opening. Cut a dollar sign from felt and glue it to the front of the purse. Run the second piece of ribbon through the handle of the purse and tie it like a sash around the cat's waist.

Cavalier Cat is ready for an adventure.

Chapter 12

Wendy Rabbit

This little rabbit looked within.
This little rabbit hopped right in!
This little rabbit came to play.
This little rabbit ran away!
This little rabbit cried, "Dear me,
Dinner is done and it's time for tea!"

Traditional Counting Rhyme

*R*ABBITS look soft and innocent; their large round eyes give them the appearance of being perpetually startled. They are often characterized as cuddly, gentle animals; but they have another side to their natures. I had a pet rabbit when I was a girl; everytime I opened his cage door, he pawed the ground, growled, and charged. If anyone attempted to stroke his velvety fur, he bit their finger. I also remember that every spring wild rabbits devoured the tender seedlings in my father's garden. For these reasons, Wendy Rabbit is saucy rather than soft, pert rather than innocent.

Wendy Rabbit's torso, her inner ears, and her legs are cut from flower-printed cotton fabric. You should accent one of the colors in the print when choosing fabric for the head, arms, outer ears, and shoes. I used lavender bonded panne velvet for them, but this fabric may be difficult to find; and velvet, velveteen, ribless corduroy, or brushed denim may be substituted. You can also substitute fabrics without a nap, but surface texture is a pleasant extra for a doll. Make her dress a bright print to contrast her body. When completed, Wendy will measure 20 inches tall.

12-1   Wendy Rabbit

MATERIALS

½ yard of fabric, preferably with a nap, for the head, outer ears, arms, and shoes.

¼ yard of printed medium-weight cotton for the shoes, torso, and inner ears.

½ yard of white cotton flannel for lining.

Scraps of felt for the eyes and mouth, and a scrap of shiny pink fabric, like satin, for the nose.

Thread to match the fabric and clear nylon thread.

Kapok or Dacron to stuff the doll.

½ yard of bright printed cotton for the dress and ruffle.

½ yard of white lace edging, ½-inch wide, for the collar and the cuffs.

A 12-inch length of white satin ribbon ½-inch wide for the waistband.

A snap closure for the dress neck edge.

A 6 × 11-inch piece of cotton fabric for the panties.

A 9-inch length of elastic ¼-inch wide.

Two bells with ½-inch diameters, each with a loop for attaching them to fabric.

Three or four small artificial flowers to tuck into the dress sash.

STEP ONE

Enlarge the patterns for the Basic Doll #1 (Fig. 12-2) and for Wendy Rabbit and her clothes (Fig. 12-3). From the fabrics you have chosen, cut the appropriate number of pieces as marked on the patterns. Transfer the X marked on the front head piece to the *wrong* side of the fabric. Transfer all other markings to the *right* side of the fabric.

Cut lining pieces for all parts of the doll body, including the shoes. Pin each lining piece to the *wrong* side of its corresponding piece.

STEP TWO

Note: ¼-inch seams allowed. Unless otherwise stated, stitch fabric with *right* sides together. Remove all pins when turning assembled pieces right side out.

Begin to assemble Wendy Rabbit by stitching together the *long straight* edge of the two *back head* pieces (Fig. 10-5a). Press this piece flat. Stitch the gusset to the back head piece between the two dots marked on the fabric (Fig. 12-4a). Next, stitch the front head pieces together, stitching from the base of the neck to the X marked below the chin. Insert the

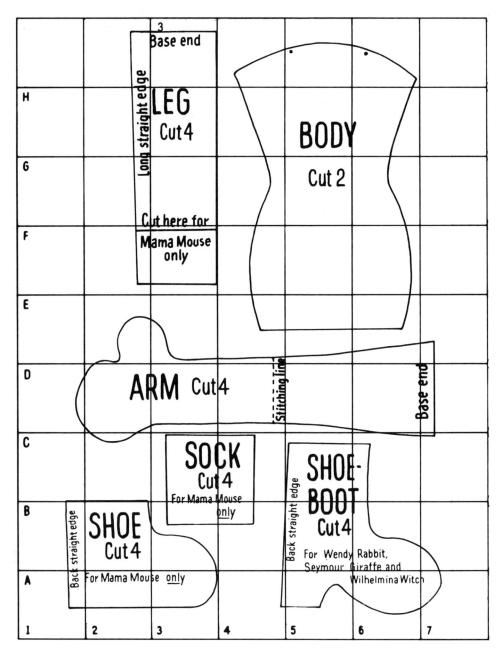

12-2 Basic Doll #1

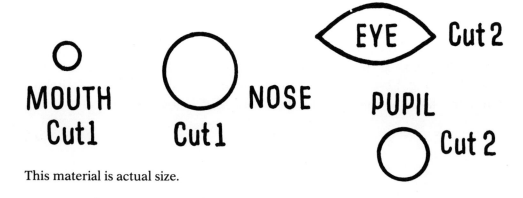

This material is actual size.

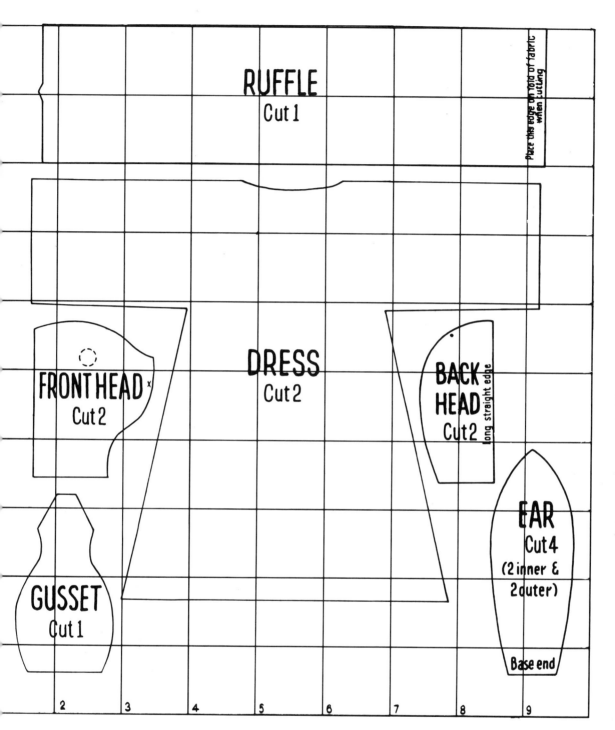

RUFFLE
Cut 1

Place this edge on fold of fabric when cutting

DRESS
Cut 2

FRONT HEAD x
Cut 2

BACK HEAD
Cut 2

long straight edge

EAR
Cut 4
(2 inner &
2 outer)

Base end

GUSSET
Cut 1

2   3   4   5   6   7   8   9

3   Wendy Rabbit

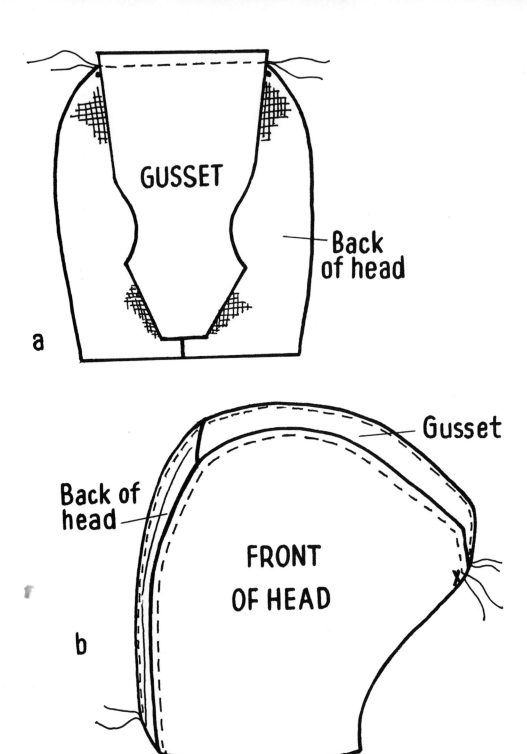

GUSSET

Back
of head

a

Gusset

Back of
head

FRONT
OF HEAD

b

12-4a. Stitching the gusset to the back of the head
   b. Stitching the gusset and the back of the head to the front of the head

Horatio Horse, Elmo Elephant, and Sir Charles Camel

Cavalier Cat and the Three Bears

Wendy Rabbit, Seymour Giraffe, and Mama and Mina Mouse

Wilhelmina Witch and Wendall Wizard

pointed tip of the gusset into the V formed by the two head pieces where they join at the X. Baste the gusset to one side of the head, beginning at the pointed tip and continuing around the head, basting the back head piece to the side of the head (Fig. 12-4b). Ease the gusset to fit the curves. Baste the second side of the gusset to the second head piece, also stitching the front head piece to the back head piece along the side seam. Now machine stitch. Trim the seams. Turn the head right side out.

Stuff the head *firmly*. Cut a circle of fabric slightly larger than the neck opening. Turn under ¼ inch of fabric around the edge. Stitch the circle of fabric over the opening, turning the raw edge under as you proceed. This scrap of fabric prevents the stuffing from escaping when you are working on other parts of the doll.

Stitch one *inner* ear to one *outer* ear, but leave the base of the ear open. Stitch the second pair of ear pieces together. Turn the ears right side out. Press. Topstitch ¼ inch within the outer edge, following the seamline of each ear.

Turn ½ inch of fabric to the inside, around the base of each ear. Stitch the base closed. Now pinch the base together, then stitch the pinch closed (Fig. 6-6b). Next stitch approximately ¼ inch of the lower portion of each ear to each side of the head. The ears should be positioned toward the back of the head, running parallel to and covering the seam that attaches the front to the back. Remember to stitch the ears securely to the head.

Stitch the two body pieces together, leaving an opening between the dots marked on the fabric. Turn the body right side out. Stuff the piece *firmly*, but leave enough room to insert the neck 1 inch into the opening. Turn under ¼ inch of fabric, around the neck edge. Insert the neck into the opening. With clear nylon thread, stitch the head fabric to the edge of the neck opening, sewing around the perimeter twice.

Stitch each pair of arm pieces together, leaving the base open. Turn the arms right side out. *Firmly* stuff the hand and the lower arm to within ½ inch of the stitching line. To make the elbow joint, sew along the stitching line twice, by hand or machine. Stuff the upper arm to within 1 inch of the open end of the arm. Turn ¼ inch of fabric to the inside, around the edges of the opening. Stitch the opening closed. Stuff the second arm, stitch the elbow joint, then stuff and stitch the base end closed. Now stitch an arm to each side of the body, at the shoulder (Fig. 15-4).

Stitch the *back straight* edge of two shoe pieces together, then press the piece open. Stitch one *long straight* edge of two of the leg pieces together, then press the piece open. Stitch the lower edge of the leg to the upper edge of the shoe (Fig. 15-5a). Now close the piece, and stitch from the top of the leg all the way around the shoe to the heel. Turn the leg right side out. Repeat and assemble the second shoe and leg.

Firmly stuff the shoe and leg to 1 inch above the top of the shoe. To make a knee joint, flatten the leg (as shown in Fig. 15-5c), and stitch across the leg twice. Continue stuffing to within 1-inch of the open end of the leg. Turn ¼ inch of fabric to the inside, around the edges of the opening. Stitch the opening closed. Stuff and stitch the second leg. Stitch the legs to the body (Fig. 15-4).

STEP THREE

Wendy's face is simple to assemble. She has bright round eyes, a shiny nose, and a pert mouth. Glue the eyes on each side of Wendy's head over the circles marked with dotted lines. Next glue a pupil to the center of each eye. After the glue has dried, stitch the eyes and pupils to the head. Paint a dab of acrylic paint in the center of each eye for a highlight or stitch a tiny triangular piece of white felt to each pupil.

Glue the tiny, round circle for Wendy's mouth to the point where the tip of the gusset joins with the two front head pieces. Stitch the mouth to the fabric.

Use a basting stitch and stitch around the perimeter of the pink circle for the nose (Fig. 11-5b). Place a tiny pad of stuffing in the center of the *wrong* side of the fabric. Pull up the stitching so that the fabric gathers around the stuffing. Place the nose, with the stuffing side down, in the center of the gusset, 1½ inches above the mouth. Stitch the edges of the nose to the head fabric.

STEP FOUR

Note: ¼-inch seams allowed.

Wendy wears a pretty dress with a lacy trim and a ruffled hem and panties under it. Begin the panties by pressing under ¼ inch on one *long* edge of the rectangular panty fabric, and stitch this pressed edge in place. Then press ¼ inch of fabric along the same edge, to the inside, and zigzag the hem in place by machine or by hand. To create a casing for the elastic, press under ¼ inch of fabric on the *opposite*, long edge of the rectangle. Stitch. Press under ¾ inch of fabric along this same edge. Stitch close to both edges of the piece you turned under. Now thread a 9-inch piece of elastic through the casing and stitch the elastic to both ends. With right sides of the fabric together, stitch the *narrow* ends of the rectangle together. Trim the seams to ⅛ inch. Turn the panties right side out and put them on Wendy with the elastic around her waist. Stitch the panties together between her legs with ten or twelve hand stitches.

Wendy Rabbit is a springtime creature, a good Easter basket surprise, and her dress should be fresh and flowery, with lots of white lace trim and

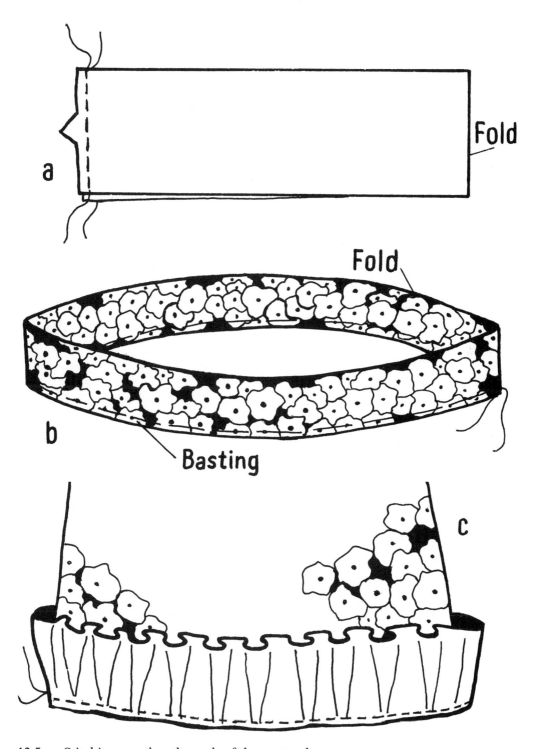

12-5a. Stitching together the ends of the rectangle
  b. Folding the piece with wrong sides together and basting along the raw edges
  c. Stitching the ruffle to the lower edge of the dress

white ribbons. Begin the dress by cutting a 2-inch slit at the neck edge of one dress piece. This will be the back of the dress. Now take the remaining dress piece and stitch it to the back dress piece at the shoulder seams (Fig. 17-3), stitching from the neck edge to the ends of the sleeves. Press ¼ inch of fabric around the neck edge and along the edges of the slit to the inside. Stitch this edge in place.

Cut a piece of lace edging ½ inch longer than the neck edge: approximately 10 inches. Stitch the lace to the right side of the dress neck, so that it lies flat to form a collar. Turn under ¼ inch of lace at each side of the slash opening, then tack it to the inside.

Turn ¼ inch of fabric to the inside, along the ends of each sleeve. Press, then stitch the fabric in place. Along these same edges, turn ½ inch of fabric to the inside and press. To form a casing for the elastic, stitch close to both sides of the folded piece on each sleeve. Cut two pieces of lace, each the length of the casing: approximately 6 inches. Stitch one piece of lace close to the end of each sleeve, being careful not to interfere with the casing. Thread a 3-inch length of ¼-inch wide elastic through each casing, then stitch the elastic to both ends of each casing.

Stitch the entire underarm seams from the tips of the sleeves to the lower edge of the dress.

Stitch together the notched ends of the ruffle fabric, so that it forms a circle (Fig. 12-5a). Fold the piece in half, with the *wrong* sides together, so that you have a narrow circle of fabric with no wrong sides visible, then press the folded piece. Next run a basting stitch the entire length of the piece, ¼ inch inside the raw edge (Fig. 12-5b). Draw up the stitching so that the piece is gathered. Pin the gathered edge to the lower edge of the dress, right sides together (Fig. 12-5c). Baste the ruffle in place and arrange the gathers so that they are even around the lower edge of the dress. Stitch the ruffle to the dress. Trim the seam. Press the ruffle down and press the dress.

Stitch a snap closure to the edges of the slash so that the dress will snap shut at the back of the doll's neck.

Tie a bow of white satin ribbon and stitch it to the center front of the dress lace collar.

Put the dress on Wendy, then tie a white satin waistband around her, and slip a sprig of artificial flowers into the band.

To suggest shoelaces, stitch a piece of bright embroidery thread through the upper side of each of Wendy's shoes, and tie the thread in a bow. Sew a bell securely behind each bow.

Wendy Rabbit is completed.

Chapter 13

Seymour Giraffe

Don't laugh at the giraffe,
It can't take the gaff.
It's sensitive as heck
Because of its long neck.

Jerome Roth

GIRAFFES are the tallest of all living mammals; some reach a height of nearly 20 feet. Because of their disproportionately long neck and legs, large ears, and quizzical faces, they look helpless and clumsy. But giraffes can defend themselves quite well with their front hoofs; and when they run in long-legged lopes, they are as graceful as basketball players. Still, they remind me of people with dreamy minds who seem constantly caught off guard. Seymour Giraffe is just such a doll: he is a lovable bumbler, an excellent toy for toddlers who recognize an equal in his uncoordinated body. His long neck also makes him easy for small hands to handle.

Seymour's head is cut from calico print cotton, but bright plaid corduroy also makes a particularly attractive doll. His mane is black rug yarn. His torso, arms, and legs are cut from orange kettle cloth, a sturdy wash-and-wear cotton fabric with a slight texture to the weave. Kettle cloth comes in a variety of clear, bright colors and is strong and wrinkle resistant; yet it is light enough to make turning narrow parts of arms and legs an easy proposition. Seymour's boots are made from vinyl leather-look fabric, but dark brown or black cotton will do. His shirt should be a flashy knit, like panne velvet or brightly printed polyester. His pants are denim and can be cut from an old pair of dungarees. His hat is felt. Seymour is 26 inches tall.

13-1   Seymour Giraffe

MATERIALS

⅓ yard of sturdy calico print or plaid corduroy for the head and outer ears.

½ yard of medium-weight fabric for the body, arms, legs, and inner ears.

⅛ yard of imitation leather or other dark-colored fabric for the boots.

½ yard of white cotton flannel for the lining.

2 yards of black rug yarn for the mane, and one yard of colorful rug yarn for the hatband.

¼ yard of bright, flashy fabric for the shirt.

¼ yard of denim for the pants.

A 6 × 11-inch piece of fabric for the panties.

A 9 × 12-inch piece of felt for the hat, and scraps of felt for the eyes and pupils.

Two 9-inch lengths of ¼-inch wide elastic.

Thread to match the fabric and clear nylon thread.

Kapok or Dacron to stuff the doll.

STEP ONE

Enlarge the patterns for the Basic Doll #1 and for Seymour and his clothes (Figs. 12-2, 13-2, and 13-3). From the fabrics you have chosen, cut the appropriate number of pieces as marked on the patterns. Transfer the stitching lines that are marked on the arm pattern to the *right* sides of the fabric. Transfer the circles for the eyes and the ear lines to the *right* side of the head fabric. Transfer all other markings to the *wrong* side of the fabric.

Cut pieces from the lining fabric for all parts of the head and body, including the shoes. Pin the lining to the wrong side of each corresponding piece.

STEP TWO

Note: ¼-inch seams allowed. Unless otherwise stated, stitch fabric with *right* sides together. Remove all pins when turning assembled pieces right side out.

Before you begin to stitch Seymour together, look carefully at Fig. 13-4, which illustrates the head assembly and placing of the mane. Lay one head piece flat on your work surface with the *right* side of the fabric facing up. Cut the black rug yarn for the mane into 2-inch lengths. Place the pieces horizontally along the neck, as close together as possible, beginning at the base of the neck and working to the X marked at the base of the head. The yarn should extend ½ inch beyond the edge of the fabric.

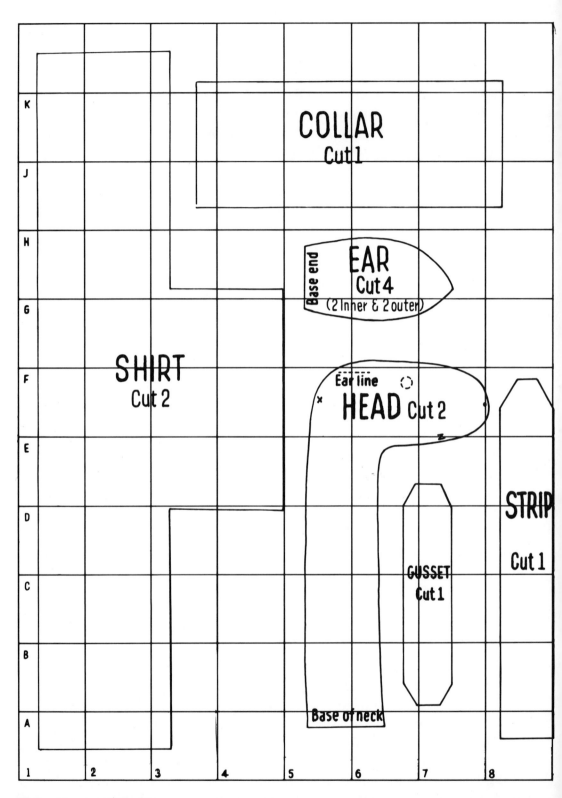

13-2   Seymour's body

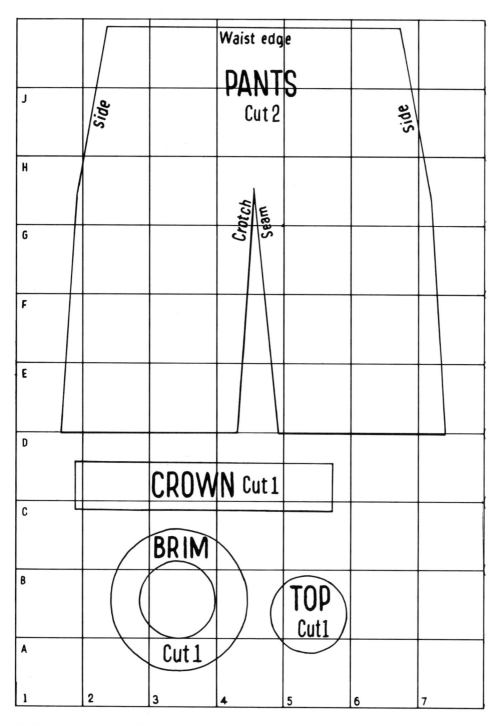

13-3   Seymour's clothing

Place the second head piece over the first, with right side together. Baste the two pieces together from the base of the neck to the X, catching in the pieces of the mane as you stitch. Next, machine stitch the two head pieces together. Trim the yarn extending beyond the seam.

To attach the gusset to the head, first place one pointed tip at the X on the head, then baste one side of the gusset to the head (Fig. 13-4b). Continue basting to the second tip that curves around and ends at the dot marked halfway down the nose. Baste the second side of the gusset to the second head piece. Stitch the gusset to the head.

Stitch together the front neck edge of the two head pieces, stitching from the dot marked on the nose to the Z marked beneath the chin (Fig. 13-4b).

Baste the strip to one head piece, placing the pointed tip in the V formed by the two head pieces under the chin (Fig. 13-4b). Stitch the strip from the Z to the base of the neck. Repeat and stitch the second side of the strip to the second head piece. Turn the head right side out. *Firmly* stuff the head and neck. Cut an oval of scrap fabric slightly larger than the opening at the base of the neck. Turn ¼ inch of fabric to the inside, around the base of the neck. Stitch the oval of fabric over the opening, turning the raw edges of the piece to the inside as you proceed. This will keep the stuffing from falling out.

Stitch one *inner* ear to one *outer* ear, leaving the base end open. Stitch the second inner ear to the second outer ear. Turn ¼ inch of fabric to the inside, around the base of each ear. Stitch the base shut. Pinch the base together, then stitch the pinch closed (Fig. 6-6b). Stitch an ear to each side of the giraffe's head, along the lines marked on each side of the head. Make sure you stitch them securely in place.

Stitch together the two body pieces, leaving an opening between the two dots marked on the shoulder edge. Turn the body right side out. Stuff it *firmly*, leaving a gap in the stuffing at the neck, so that there is room to insert the neck 1 inch. Now insert the neck. Turn ¼ inch of fabric around the edge of the body opening to the inside. Stitch the neck securely to this turned edge. Stitch around the perimeter at least twice: Seymour's neck needs to be securely attached as children often carry him around by it.

There are four arm pieces, two for each arm. Stitch each pair together, leaving the base end open. Turn the arms right side out. Stuff the hand and lower arm *firmly* to within ½ inch of the stitching line. To create an elbow joint, stitch across the line twice with your sewing machine. Continue to stuff the arm to within 1 inch of the open end. Turn ¼ inch of fabric to the inside, around the edges of the opening. Stitch the opening shut. Stitch an arm to each side of Seymour's body (Fig. 15-4).

Begin to attach the boots to the legs by first stitching together the *back straight* edge of one pair of boot pieces. Press the leg and boot open and

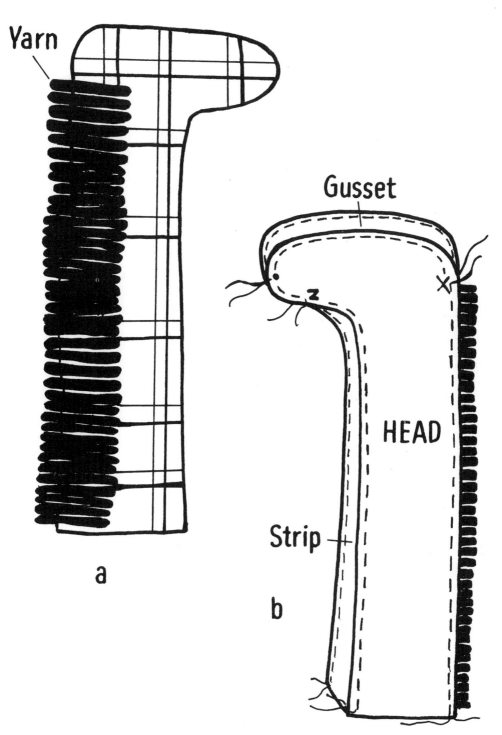

Yarn

Gusset

HEAD

Strip

a

b

13-4a. Placing pieces of yarn for the mane side by side along the neck
   b. Stitching the gusset and strip to the head and stitching together the two
       head pieces

flat. Stitch the *upper* edge of the boot to the *lower* edge of the leg (Fig. 15-5). Close the leg and the boot. Stitch from the upper edge of the leg, all the way around the piece, to the heel of the shoe. Stitch together the second leg and boot. Turn both assembled pieces right side out. *Firmly* stuff the boot and lower leg to 1 inch above the top of the boot. To create a knee joint, flatten the leg (Fig. 15-5c), then stitch across it twice. Continue to stuff above the joint to within 1 inch of the upper end of the leg. Turn ¼ inch of fabric to the inside, around the edge of the base opening. Stitch the opening shut. Stuff and stitch the second leg. Stitch both legs to the body (Fig. 15-4).

STEP THREE

Seymour's features are not elaborate. He has a simple appealing face, slightly shaded by his floppy hat. Glue a pupil to each eye, and glue an eye to each side of the head, over the circles marked on the fabric. After the glue has dried, stitch the eyes and pupils to the head. For a highlight, paint a dab of white acrylic in the center of each eye, or glue and stitch a small triangle of white felt to each pupil.

STEP FOUR

Note: ¼-inch seams allowed.

Seymour's clothes establish his bumbling, dreamy personality; his soft flamboyant shirt, his baggy jeans, and floppy hat give him a helpless appearance.

Underpants are a part of a child's everyday life, and I think a doll should be as much like a child as possible. Seymour's panties will suit his personality if they are cut from bold geometric print or a splashy flowered fabric. Begin the panties by pressing under ¼ inch of fabric on the *long* edge. Stitch the pressed edge down. Turn ¼ inch of fabric along the same edge to the inside and press. Zigzag stitch this piece in place or hem by hand. To make a casing for the elastic, first press under ¼ inch of fabric along the *opposite* long edge, then stitch it in place. Press ¾ inch of fabric to the inside along this same edge. Stitch close to both edges of the piece that's turned under. Now thread a 9-inch length of ¼ inch wide elastic through the casing and stitch it to the fabric at both ends. Stitch the narrow ends of the rectangle together. Trim the seam to ⅛ inch. Turn the panties right side out and press. Put them on Seymour with the elastic around his waist. Stitch the fabric together between his legs with several hand stitches.

To assemble Seymour's shirt, start by stitching the underarm seams from the lower edge of the shirt to the tips of the sleeves (Fig. 17-3). Stitch the shoulder seams from the ends of the sleeves to the dot marked on the shoulder. Hem the sleeves and the lower edge of the shirt by hand or machine, turning under ½ inch of fabric along these edges. Turn the shirt right side out and press; then put it on the doll by slipping it over his head.

To make the shirt collar, press the rectangular piece of fabric in half, so that it is long and narrow; then stitch the narrow ends together (Fig. 15-7a). Turn the collar right side out and press. Next turn ¼ inch of shirt fabric to the inside around the neck edge. Wrap the collar around the doll's neck so that the raw edge is underneath the shirt neckline and the ends of the collar meet at the back of his neck (Fig. 15-7b). By hand, stitch the ends of the collar together where they meet at the back of the neck. Stitch the collar to the shirt neck. Fold the collar down to create a turtleneck.

To make Seymour's jeans, begin by joining two pieces together on one side, from the waist to the end of the leg. Press ¼ inch of fabric along the waist edge to the inside. Stitch the edge in place. Press under ¾ inch of fabric along this same edge. Now stitch close to both edges of this folded piece to form a casing for the elastic. Thread a 9-inch length of ¼-inch wide elastic through the casing, then stitch it securely to both ends. Stitch together the remaining side seam of the pants. Now stitch the entire crotch seam, then turn the pants right side out and press. Try the pants on the doll and turn up the legs to a proper length; then remove the pants, hem the legs by hand, and put them back on the doll.

Because Seymour's floppy hat is made of felt, it is glued together rather than stitched. Before starting work on the hat, look carefully at the assembly steps illustrated in Fig. 11-5a. First form a cylinder by overlapping the ends of the rectangular piece of felt 1 inch, and glue the overlap together. Allow the glue to dry, then glue the circular piece of felt over one edge of the cylinder. Again allow the glue to dry, then coat the rim of the remaining open end of the cylinder with glue. Slip the brim of the hat over the crown, downward over the rim of glue. Turn the hat upside down and support the brim with thread spools so that it will dry without sticking to the table.

Crochet a chain of yarn of sufficient length to tie around the crown of the hat for a hatband (Fig. 7-4b). Place the knot in the back at the seam of the crown. Allow two 2-inch lengths of unchained yarn to dangle and unravel them for a decorative effect. Stitch an 8-inch length of rug yarn through the brim, the hatband, and the crown, approximately 1½ inches forward of the center back of the hat. Tie the piece of yarn in a knot inside the hat so that it is concealed. Stitch another 8-inch length of yarn in the same position on the opposite side of the hat. Put the hat on Seymour's head. The yarn ties should cross in front of the left ear and behind the right ear. Tie the yarn in a bow beneath his chin.

Seymour Giraffe is ready to play.

Chapter 14

Mama and Mina Mouse

The city mouse lives in a house;
   The garden mouse lives in a bower,
He's friendly with the frogs and toads,
   And sees the pretty plants in flower.
The City Mouse and the Garden Mouse
Christina Georgina Rossetti

*M*ICE are not welcome in the average household, and their departure is usually hastened by whatever means are available. But mice who live out of doors are treated much differently than their indoor relations. Deer mice, for example, have limpid eyes, large ears, and dainty feet. They are easily tamed when bribed with bits of food. A more innocent and gentle looking creature would be hard to find.

Mama Mouse and her diapered offspring, Mina, are descended from the outdoor branch of the mouse family. Mama Mouse is old-fashioned, the paragon of cleanliness and neatness; a temperamental relative of Mrs. Tittlemouse, the Beatrix Potter creation. The baby mouse is made entirely of felt, and the mother mouse's head and arms are also cut from felt. Soft felt gives a doll a pleasant surface texture; but because it's a pressed fabric, it must be lined or it will pull apart. I made Mama Mouse's head and arms white, but bright yellow, brown, grey, or any warm color of felt will work as well. Her body and legs are cut from a cotton fabric, as are her panties, dress, and apron. When dressing a doll, it is fun to mix prints. Pink and blue go very nicely for Mama Mouse. When completed, she will measure 23 inches, and Mina will measure 6 inches.

14-1　Mama and Mina Mouse

MATERIALS

⅓ yard of felt for the head, arms, outer ears, and socks of Mama Mouse and for the body and outer ears of Mina Mouse.

One 9 × 12-inch rectangle of pink felt for the inner ears of both mice and for the baby's diaper.

¼ yard of bright, printed cotton for the body and shoes of Mama Mouse.

½ yard of white cotton flannel to line Mama Mouse.

A 9-inch length of ¼-inch wide elastic.

A 6 × 11-inch rectangle of fabric for Mama's panties.

⅓ yard of print cotton fabric for Mama's dress.

¼ yard of a different cotton print for Mama's apron.

1 yard of ½-inch wide white lace edging for Mama's apron.

2 yards of ½-inch wide red satin ribbon also for Mama's apron.

A 12-inch length of ¼-inch wide pastel colored satin ribbon to tie in a bow around Mina Mouse's neck.

Scraps of yellow and black felt for the eyes and pupils of both mice.

Approximately 1½ yards of bright embroidery thread for the shoelaces.

One black, ball-shaped button with a ½-inch diameter for Mama Mouse's nose.

One snap closure, for the back neck opening of Mama Mouse's dress.

Thread to match the fabric and clear nylon thread.

Kapok or Dacron to stuff the dolls.

STEP ONE

Enlarge the patterns for the Basic Doll #1 and for Mama and Mina Mouse and their clothes (Figs. 12-2 and 14-2). From the fabrics you have chosen, cut the appropriate number of pieces as marked on the patterns. Transfer the markings for the stitching lines on the arms, the X's for the ears, and the circles for Mama Mouse's eyes to the *right* side of the fabric. Transfer the circles for placement of Mina Mouse's eyes to the *right* side of *one* body piece only. Transfer all other markings to the wrong side of the fabric.

Cut lining pieces for Mama Mouse's body parts, including her shoes. It is not necessary to cut lining pieces for Mama Mouse's ears or for any part of Mina Mouse. Pin the lining pieces to the *wrong* side of the corresponding pieces cut previously.

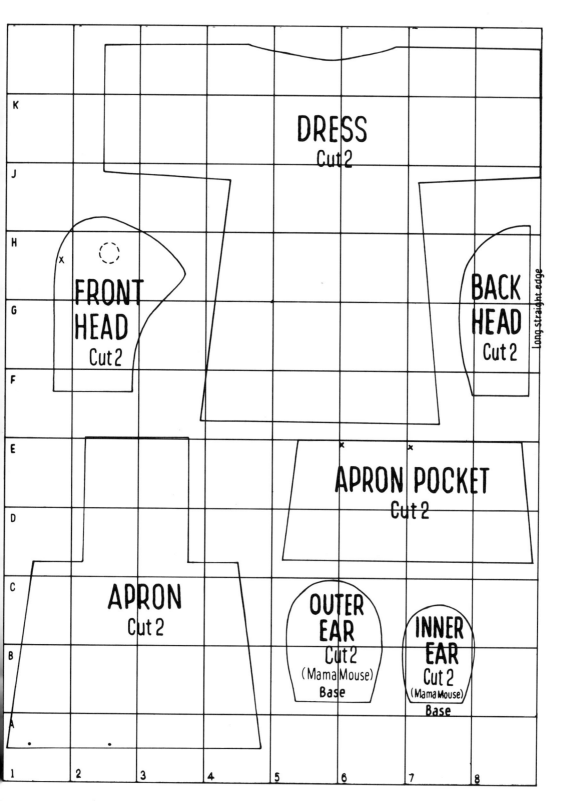

14-2   Mama and Mina Mouse

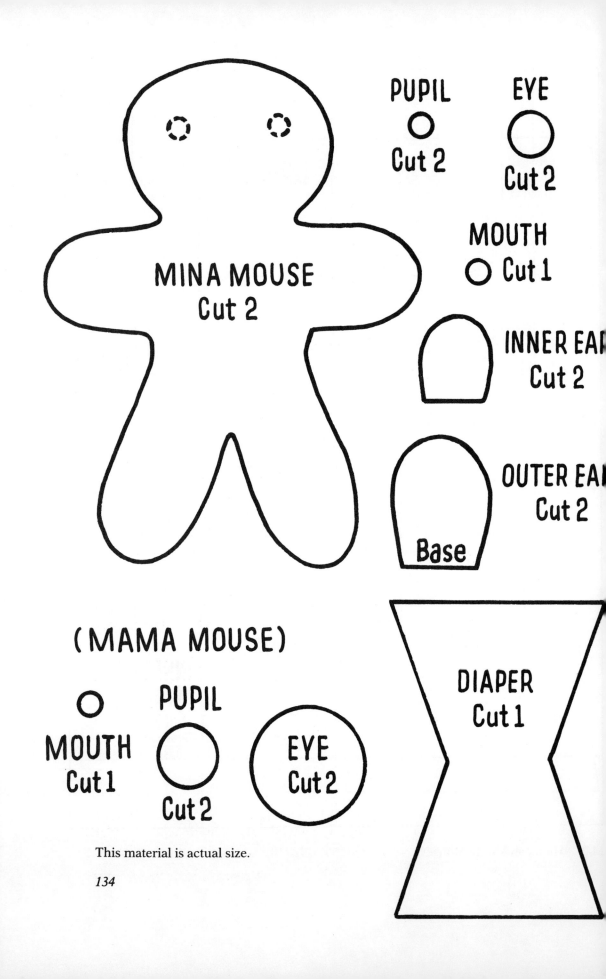

PUPIL
Cut 2

EYE
Cut 2

MOUTH
Cut 1

INNER EAR
Cut 2

OUTER EAR
Cut 2

MINA MOUSE
Cut 2

Base

DIAPER
Cut 1

(MAMA MOUSE)

PUPIL

MOUTH
Cut 1

Cut 2

EYE
Cut 2

This material is actual size.

134

> *Note:* ¼-inch seams allowed. Unless otherwise stated, stitch fabric with *right* sides together. Remove all pins when turning assembled pieces right side out.

Start with Mama Mouse. Stitch together the two front head pieces from the lower front edge of the neck, around the nose, to the back of the head (Fig. 14-3b). Leave the back edge of the head unstitched.

Stitch together the long *straight* edge of the back pieces (Fig. 14-3a). Press the piece open and flat. Baste the curved edge of the assembled back head piece to the back edge of the front head piece (Fig. 14-3c). Align the center seams. Stitch the pieces together. Trim the neck edge. Turn the head right side out.

Firmly stuff the head, making sure to get some stuffing up into the tip of the nose. Cut an oval of scrap fabric slightly larger than the neck opening, then stitch it over the opening, turning the raw edges to the inside as you stitch. This will keep the stuffing from falling out.

Glue a pink felt *inner* ear to each *outer* ear. After the glue has dried, topstitch ¼ inch inside the outer edge of the inner ear. Pinch the base of each ear shut (Fig. 6-6b). Stitch an ear to each side of Mama Mouse's head, over the X marked on the fabric.

Stitch the two body pieces together, stitching around the perimeter; but leave an opening between the two dots marked on the shoulder edge of the piece. Turn the body right side out and stuff it *firmly*, but leave enough room to insert the neck.

Turn ¼ inch of fabric around the neck edge to the inside. Insert the neck. Stitch the neck fabric to the body neck edge. Stitch the pieces securely to one another.

There are four arm pieces, two for each arm. Stitch each pair together around the perimeter, leaving the base end open. Turn the arms right side out. *Firmly* stuff the hand and lower arm to within ½ inch of the stitching line. To create an elbow joint, stitch across the stitching line twice, by hand or by machine. Stuff the remainder of the arm to within 1 inch of the open end. Turn ½ inch of fabric to the inside around the opening and stitch the opening shut. Now stitch an arm to each side of the doll's body (Fig. 15-4).

Mama Mouse's shoes, socks, and legs are assembled together to form one piece. Begin by stitching together the *back straight* edge of two shoe pieces. Press the piece open and flat. Stitch together the *straight* edge of two sock pieces. Press this piece open. Stitch the upper edge of the shoe to the lower edge of the sock, aligning the seams. Stitch together the *long straight* edge of two leg pieces. Press this piece open. Stitch the upper edge of the sock to the lower edge of the leg (Fig. 15-5). Close the piece, aligning

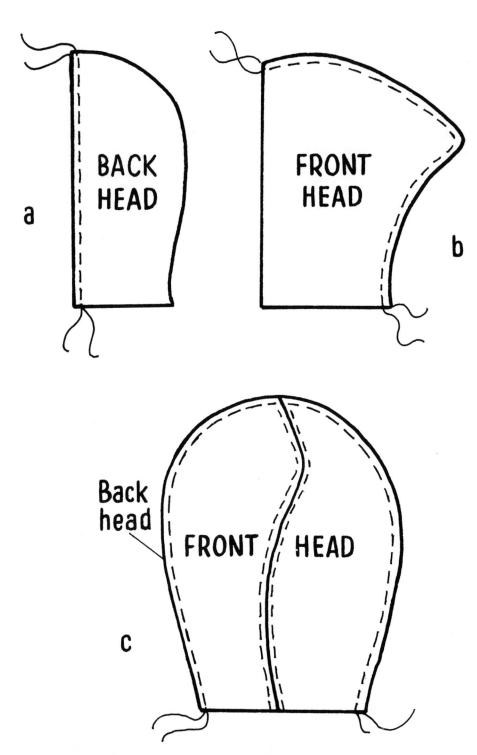

14-3a. Stitching together the two back head pieces
   b. Stitching together the two front head pieces
   c. Stitching the front of the head to the back of the head

each of the seams and the top of the shoe. Stitch from the upper edge of the leg, down the front of the piece, around to the heel of the shoe. Repeat this procedure, assembling the second leg, sock, and shoe. Turn both pieces right side out.

Stuff the shoe, sock, and lower leg to 1 inch above the sock. To create a knee joint, flatten the leg as illustrated in Fig. 15-5c and stitch across the leg twice. Continue stuffing above the joint to within 1 inch of the open end. Turn ½ inch of fabric to the inside around the edges of the opening and stitch the opening shut. Stuff and stitch a knee joint on the second leg. Stitch both legs to the body (Fig. 15-4).

Glue a pink *inner* ear to each of Mina Mouse's *outer* ears. After the glue has dried, topstitch the inner ear to each outer ear, placing the stitching ¼ inch within the edge of the inner ear.

Now for Mina Mouse. Because she is tiny, it would be difficult to stitch her together and then turn her right side out. Consequently, she is made of felt; and since there are no raw edges, she is topstitched together. First, insert the ears between the head pieces, so that the base of each ear is covered by ½ inch of fabric (Fig. 14-4a). The ears may be basted in position with a few hand stitches. Then topstitch together the two body pieces, stitching around the head, arms, and legs of the doll, catching in the ears, but leaving a 1-inch wide opening in the side of one leg for stuffing. Next stuff the doll through this opening, pushing only little wads of stuffing at a time. Stuff the doll enough to gently fill out the forms. Too firm a stuffing job will tear the felt. When you have finished stuffing, close the 1-inch opening with topstitching.

STEP THREE

To give Mama Mouse real character, she needs a black shiny nose and two large wide eyes. Stitch the black ball-shaped button to the tip of her nose. Stitch the button especially secure, so that it can not be chewed loose by a young child.

Glue an eye to each side of Mama Mouse's head, over the circles marked on the fabric. Glue a pupil to each eye. Stitch the eye to the head and the pupil to the eye. Paint a dab of white acrylic in the center of each eye or glue a small dot of white felt to each pupil and stitch it in position.

Glue the mouth to the underside of the head, over the seamline. Stitch it in place.

Glue Mina Mouse's eyes to her head, over the circles marked on the fabric for placement. Glue the pupils to the eyes and the tiny pink felt mouth to the head. Stitch each of these features to her face.

Tie a piece of pastel ribbon in a bow around Mina Mouse's neck. Next

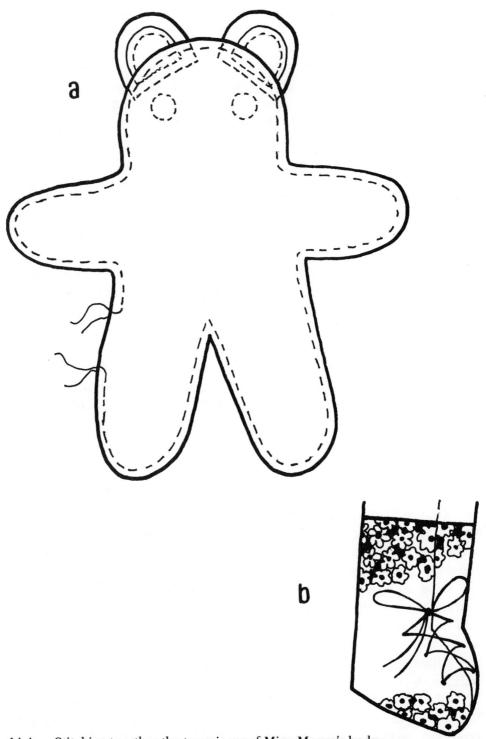

14-4a. Stitching together the two pieces of Mina Mouse's body
    b. Stitching embroidery thread laces to the shoe

put the felt diaper on Mina Mouse, then stitch the corners together at the points where a baby's diaper ordinarily would be fastened.

STEP FOUR

Note: ¼-inch seams allowed.

Mama Mouse's clothes are simply designed and ideally suited for ginghams, calico, or flowered cotton prints. A zigzag or other decorative machine stitch adds a nice touch to the hems on the sleeves and at the lower edge of the dress.

Make Mama Mouse's panties first. A bright piece of any scrap fabric measuring 6 × 11 inches will do. Press under ¼ inch on one *long* edge of the fabric. Stitch the pressed edge down. Turn another ¼ inch of fabric along the same edge to the inside. Use a zigzag stitch to fix the hem in place or hem by hand. Press under ¼ inch of fabric on the *opposite* long edge of the piece, and stitch the pressed edge in place. Press under ¾ inch of fabric along the same edge. To create a casing for the elastic, stitch close to both sides of this piece, then thread a 9-inch length of ¼-inch wide elastic through the casing, and stitch it securely to both ends of the casing. With right sides of the fabric together, stitch the narrow ends of the piece together, then trim the seams to ⅛ inch. Turn the panties right side out and press. Put the panties on the doll, the elastic around its waist; then with ten or twelve hand stitches, stitch them together between her legs.

Begin Mama Mouse's dress by cutting a 2-inch slash from the neck edge down the center back of *one* dress piece; this piece is the back piece. Now stitch the shoulder seams of the front dress piece to the back dress piece, from the neck edge to the ends of the sleeves (Fig. 17-3). Press ¼ inch of fabric to the inside, around the neck edge and along the edges of the slit you cut in the back dress piece. Machine stitch or hand stitch the turned edge in place. Press ¼ inch of fabric to the inside along the ends of each sleeve, and machine or hand stitch these edges in place. Stitch the underarm seams. Narrowly hem the lower edge of the dress. Turn the dress right side out and press. Sew a snap near the upper edge of the back slash at the neckline closing. Put the dress on Mama Mouse.

To make Mama Mouse's apron, with right sides together, stitch the two apron pieces together; but leave an opening between the two dots marked on the lower edge of the apron (Fig. 14-5a). Trim the seam to ⅛ inch. Turn the piece right side out through the opening. Press the apron, folding ⅛ inch of fabric to the inside along the edges of the opening.

Stitch the two pieces of the pocket together, leaving an opening between the two X's marked on the fabric. Trim the seams to ⅛ inch. Turn the pocket right side out and press, folding ⅛ inch of fabric to the inside along the edges of the opening. Cut a piece of lace edging the length of the upper edge of the pocket, approximately 7 inches; then stitch it to the edge of the pocket, sewing the edges of the opening shut as you do so. Align the pocket to the lower corner of the apron and pin it in place (Fig. 14-5b). Baste the pocket to the apron, then remove the pins.

Cut a length of lace edging, measuring approximately 18 inches, then stitch it around the perimeter of the lower half of the apron (Fig. 14-5b). During this procedure, the pocket will simultaneously be stitched to the apron. Cut another length of lace, measuring approximately 3 inches, then stitch it to the top edge of the apron.

Cut two 15-inch lengths of ½-inch wide satin ribbon. Baste one piece to each *side* of the top half of the apron, so that it extends ½ inch into the lower half of the apron (Fig. 14-5b). Then stitch the ribbons to the apron, running two rows of stitching side by side along the length of each piece. Cut a 25-inch length of ribbon and baste it horizontally across the top of the lower half of the apron, so that 9 inches of ribbon extends beyond the apron on each side (Fig. 14-5b). Baste this piece of ribbon over the ends of the other two pieces of ribbon you previously stitched to the apron. Run two lines of stitching side by side and stitch the ribbon to the apron. Put the apron on Mama Mouse, tying one set of ribbons around her waist and the other set around her neck. Put Mina Mouse in Mama's pocket.

Embroider thread laces to Mama Mouse's shoes (Fig. 14-4b).

Mama and Mina Mouse are ready for a romp in the country.

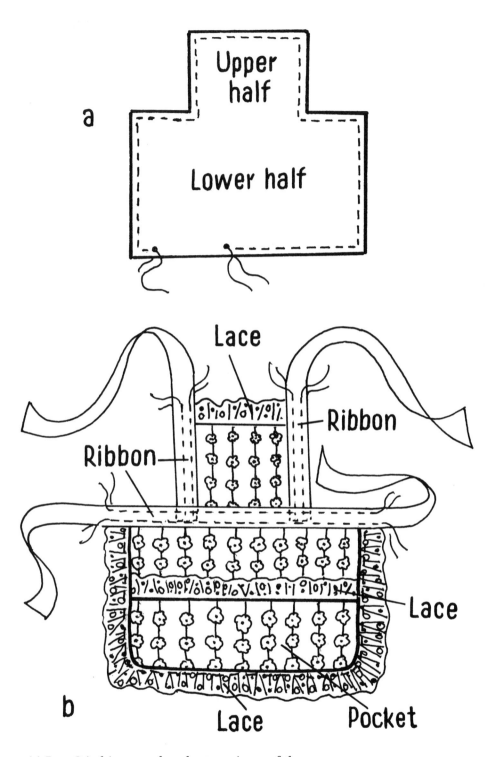

14-5a. Stitching together the two pieces of the apron
    b. Stitching the pocket, lace, and ribbons to the apron

Chapter 15

Wilhelmina Witch

"Which road leads to the Wicked Witch of the West?" asked Dorothy. "There is no road," answered the Guardian of the Gates. "No one ever wishes to go that way."

The Wizard of Oz
L. Frank Baum

*T*HE fairy tale witch is capable of a multitude of spells. She can turn a prince into a frog and make a princess sleep hundreds of years. She has been known to thwart true love and place impossible obstacles in the paths of bold adventurers; but she can be overcome by courage, inventiveness, and goodheartedness. The fairy tale witch had her origins in Europe, the British Isles in particular. As more civilized people from the Mediterranean shores advanced north, they found small-statured, brown-skinned people who lived in earthen, mound-like huts. These people were herdsmen, and they paid homage to trees, to the full moon, and to certain animals. Most of the herdsmen were eventually assimilated into the new culture, but some groups withdrew into seclusion and secretly preserved their rites. These ceremonies were misinterpreted and distorted by outsiders and gave rise to many of the misconceptions that the Middle Ages incorporated into their witchcraft mythology.

Wilhelmina Witch is a floppy, comical creature, only vaguely related to the witches of the past. I usually cut her body from red ribless corduroy and her shoes from a red and blue cotton print. Her wild hair is golden yellow mohair yarn. Her cape and skirt are navy blue cotton. Her shirt is bright plaid. She measures 22 inches.

15-1   Wilhelmina Witch

MATERIALS

½ yard of plain, medium-weight cotton fabric for the doll body.

⅛ yard of printed medium-weight cotton fabric for the shoes, and a 7 × 11-inch piece of fabric of the same kind for the cape lining.

½ yard of white cotton flannel for the lining.

One skein of bright mohair yarn for the hair.

Scraps of felt for the features.

Kapok or Dacron for stuffing.

Thread to match the fabric and clear nylon thread.

An 11 × 12-inch piece of medium-weight cotton fabric for the skirt, and a 7 × 11-inch piece of the same fabric for the cape.

¼ yard of bright cotton fabric for the shirt.

A 6 × 11-inch piece of fabric for the panties.

A 9 × 12-inch piece of felt for the hat.

Two 9-inch lengths of ¼-inch wide elastic.

A 14-inch length of colorful rug yarn.

STEP ONE

Enlarge the patterns for the Basic Doll #1 (Fig. 12-2) and for the witch and her clothes (Fig. 15-2). From the fabrics you have chosen, cut the appropriate number of pieces as marked on the patterns. Transfer all markings to the *right* side of the fabric.

Cut lining pieces for all parts of the doll body and pin them to the *wrong* side of the corresponding pieces.

STEP TWO

Note: ¼-inch seams allowed. Unless otherwise stated, stitch fabric with *right* sides together. Remove all pins when turning assembled pieces right side out.

Begin by sewing the two nose pieces together, but leave the base end *open.* Turn the nose right side out. *Lightly* stuff it to within 1 inch of the open

PUPIL
Cut 2

EYE
Cut 2

MOUT
Cut 1

This material is actual size.

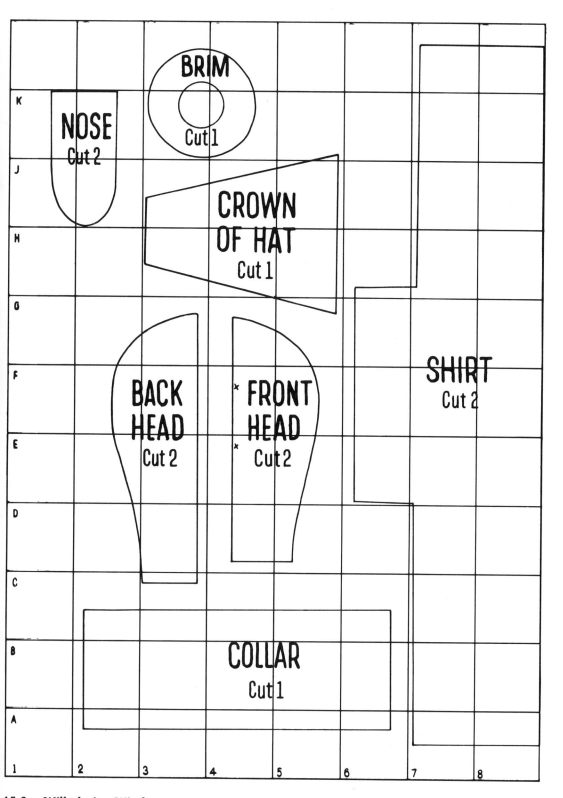

15-2   Wilhelmina Witch

end. Position the nose between the two X's marked on the front head piece, the base end extending ½ inch beyond the straight edge of the head piece (Fig. 15-3).

Stitch together the *straight* edge of two front head pieces with the nose between them. Set this piece aside and stitch together the *curved* edge of the two back head pieces. Now stitch the *curved* edge of the *front* head pieces to the *straight* edge of the *back* head pieces, easing to fit.

Trim the neck edge even. Turn the head right side out. *Firmly* stuff the head. Cut a circle slightly larger than the neck opening from a scrap of fabric; turn under ¼-inch of this fabric around the neck edge; then stitch it over the opening by hand to prevent stuffing from escaping.

Stitch together the two body pieces, leaving an opening between the two dots marked on the fabric. Turn the body right side out and stuff it *firmly*, but leave enough room to insert the neck 1 inch into the opening. Turn under ¼ inch of fabric around the edges of the opening. Insert the neck and then stitch it by hand with clear nylon thread to the edge of the opening. Stitch again to ensure strength.

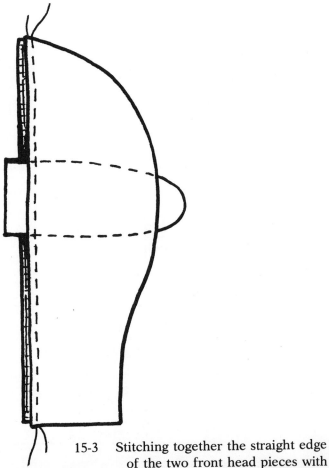

15-3   Stitching together the straight edge of the two front head pieces with the nose between them

Stitch together two of the arm pieces, leaving the base end open. Turn the arm right side out. *Firmly* stuff the hand and arm to within ½ inch of the stitching line; then stitch along the stitching line twice. Continue stuffing to within 1 inch of the open end of the arm. Turn under ¼ inch of fabric around the opening, then stitch the opening shut by hand with clear nylon thread. Repeat and assemble the second arm, then stitch the arms to the body (Fig. 15-4).

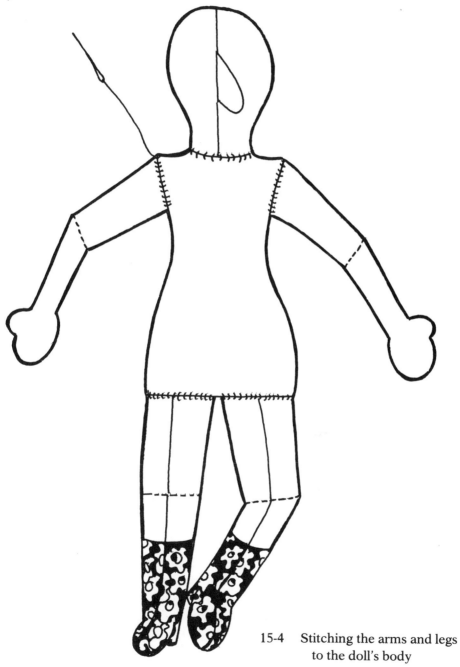

15-4   Stitching the arms and legs to the doll's body

Stitch together the *back straight* edge of one pair of shoe pieces. Stitch together the *straight* edge of two leg pieces. Press open the leg and shoe. Stitch the lower edge of the leg to the upper edge of the shoe (Fig. 15-5a). Close the assembled piece and stitch from the top of the leg all the way around to the heel of the shoe (Fig. 15-5b). Turn the piece right side out. *Firmly* stuff the shoe and leg to 1 inch above the top of the shoe. Flatten the leg, as shown in Fig. 15-5c; then stitch across the leg to create a knee joint. Continue stuffing to within 1 inch of the opening. Turn under ¼ inch of fabric around the open edge. With clear nylon thread, stitch the opening shut by hand. Repeat the entire procedure and assemble the second leg. Stitch the legs to the body (Fig. 15-5c).

STEP THREE

Wilhelmina's hair and features are essential to her character as a witch. Mohair yarn is perfect for her hair. It has a frightening, electric appearance. First roughly map out an area 2-inches square on the crown of the doll's head. Then, using a needle with a large eye, cover the area with 6-inch strands of mohair yarn, stitching and knotting the strands at the center (Fig. 15-6).

Pin the features to the face in a position you find pleasing. Cut two tiny triangular pieces of white felt for highlights. Use liquid latex or a cloth glue; and glue the highlight to the pupil, the pupil to the eye, and the eye to the head. Repeat for the second eye. When the glue has dried, stitch the features to the head with clear nylon thread.

STEP FOUR

You can use lace, ribbon, trimming, sequins, or buttons to spruce up Wilhelmina's costume and make her truly unique.

Press under ¼ inch on the *long* edge of the fabric you have chosen for the doll's panties and stitch. Turn under another ¼ inch of fabric and either zigzag the hem in place or sew it by hand. Press under ¼ inch of fabric on the *opposite* long edge and stitch. To create a casing for the elastic, press under ¾ inch of fabric along the same edge; then stitch close to both edges of the folded piece. Next thread a 9-inch length of elastic through the casing and stitch the elastic to both ends of the casing. With right sides of the fabric together, stitch the *narrow* ends of the fabric strip together. Trim the seam to ⅛ inch. Turn the panties right side out and put the panties on the doll with the elastic around her waist. With ten or twelve hand stitches, stitch the panties together between the doll's legs.

To make Wilhelmina's skirt, follow the same procedures indicated above for her panties, but, of course, omit the stitches between her legs.

Baby Karen and Grandma Sally

Crawdon Crocodile and Cyrus Centaur

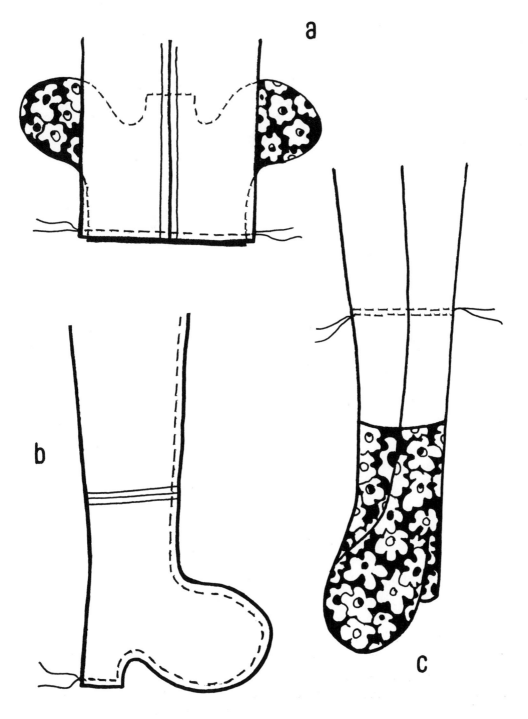

15-5a. Stitching the lower edge of the leg to the upper edge of the shoe
   b. Stitching from the top of the leg all the way round to the heel of the shoe
   c. Stitching across the leg to create a knee joint

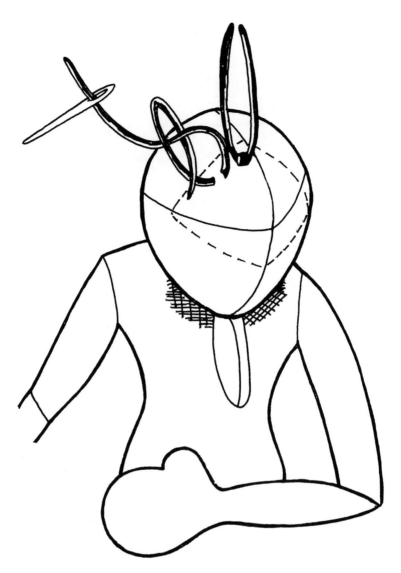

15-6   Stitching the yarn hair to the crown of the doll's head

For Wilhelmina's shirt, first stitch together the underarm seams of the two shirt pieces (Fig. 17-3). Next, stitch from the dot marked on the shoulder to the end of the sleeve. Narrowly hem the base of the shirt and the sleeves. Turn the shirt right side out, press, and slip the shirt over the doll's head.

Now take the rectangle for the shirt collar and press it in half, so that it forms a long *narrow* piece. Stitch the short ends together (Fig. 15-7a). Turn the piece right side out and press. Turn under ¼ inch of fabric around the shirt neck edge. Now wrap the collar around the doll's neck so that the raw edge is underneath the shirt neckline and the ends of the collar meet at the back of the neck (Fig. 15-7b). By hand, stitch the ends of the collar together, then stitch the collar to the shirt neck. Fold the collar down.

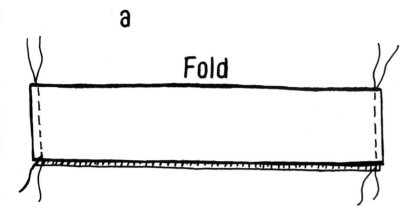

a

Fold

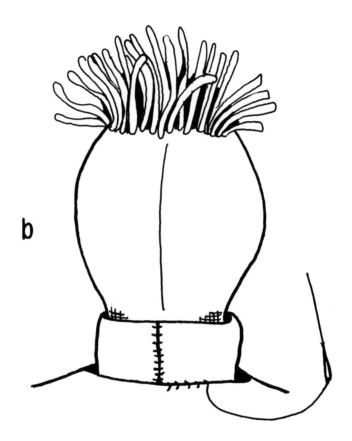

b

15-7a. Stitching together the short ends of the folded collar
  b. Stitching the collar to the shirt

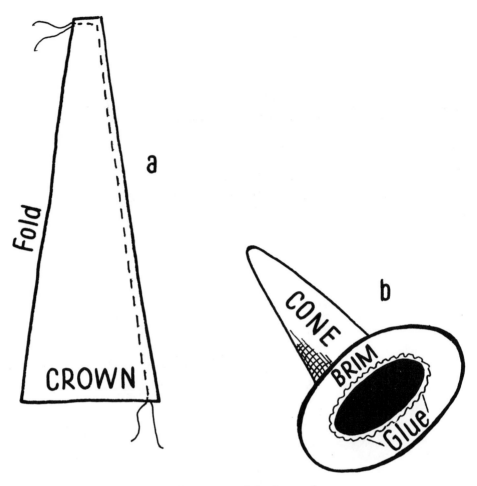

15-8a. Stitching together the crown of the hat to form a cone
b. Gluing the brim to the base of the cone

With right sides together, stitch the cape lining to the cape, but leave a 2-inch opening between the two dots marked on the fabric. Turn the cape right side out and press under ¼ inch of fabric along the edges of the opening. Top stitch around the entire perimeter of the cape, as close to the edge as possible. To form a casing, press ½ inch of fabric to the inside, along the neck edge of the cape. Stitch close to both edges of the folded piece. Thread a 14-inch length of rug yarn through the casing. Tie the yarn in a tight bow around the doll's neck, gathering up the cape as you do so. Turn up the lower corners of the cape to show off the lining.

Stitch together the crown of Wilhelmina's hat to form a cone (Fig. 15-8a). Turn the piece right side out. Glue the brim to the base of the cone with liquid latex or cloth glue (Fig. 15-8b). Stitch the hat to her head.

Hocus-pocus! Wilhelmina is ready!

Chapter 16

Wendall Wizard

Him, the most famous man of all those times,
Merlin, who knew the range of all their arts,
Had built the King his havens, ships, and halls,
Was also Bard, and knew the starry heavens;
The people call'd him Wizard....

Merlin and Vivien
Alfred Lord Tennyson

WIZARDS are magicians with good reputations. They are skillful in the arts of sorcery, but their wisdom has been tempered by age and they rarely abuse their magical powers. Every king worth his crown has a wizard nearby for consultation.

Like most of his predecessors, Wendall the Wizard has soulful and worldly wise eyes. His gown and cloak are decorated with magical symbols. I used red velvet for the gown and a bright pink satin lining for the cloak. His underpants are cut from a bright splashy print. Wendall's hair and beard are white mohair yarn flecked with grey. Keep a watchful eye when you visit yarn stores. They often sell odds and ends of yarn at reduced price, and you need only part of a skein for a whole head of hair. From the crown of his head to the bottom of his feet, Wendall measures 26 inches.

16-1   Wendall Wizard

MATERIALS

1 yard of medium-weight fabric for the body, head, arms, legs, base, ears, and nose.

¼ yard of print fabric, such as velveteen, for the hat, shoes, and the soles of the shoes.

1 yard of white cotton flannel to line the doll.

1 yard of velvet for the gown.

¼ yard of fabric for the cloak.

¼ yard of satin or taffeta to line the cloak.

A 9 × 20-inch rectangle of fabric for the panties.

A 12-inch length of 1-inch wide elastic.

Several yards of mohair yarn for the hair, mustache, and beard.

Scraps of felt in various colors for his features and for the symbol appliqués on his clothes.

A 24-inch length of 1-inch wide ribbon for the cloak tie.

Two bells with ½-inch diameters and loops to attach them to the shoes.

A snap closure for the dress.

Thread to match the fabric and clear nylon thread.

Kapok or Dacron to stuff the doll.

STEP ONE

Enlarge the patterns for the Basic Doll # 2 (Fig. 16-2) and for Wendall and his clothes (Fig. 16-3 and 16-4). From the fabrics you have chosen, cut the appropriate number of pieces as marked on the patterns. Transfer the dots marked on the arms and cloak and the X marked on the shoes to the *wrong* side of the fabric. Transfer the markings for the bird to the *right* side of the cloak fabric. Transfer all other markings to the *right* side of the fabric.

Cut lining pieces for all parts of the doll body, including the shoes, but not the soles. Pin a lining piece to the *wrong* side of each corresponding piece.

STEP TWO

Note: ¼-inch seams allowed. Unless otherwise stated, stitch with *right* sides together. Remove all pins before turning assembled pieces right side out.

Begin Wendall by assembling the various parts of his head. First stitch the two pieces of his nose together, leaving the base end open. Turn the nose right side out and stuff it *lightly* to within 1 inch of the open end. Pin the nose to the right side of one head piece, positioning it between the two X's marked on the fabric (Fig. 16-5a). The base end of the nose should

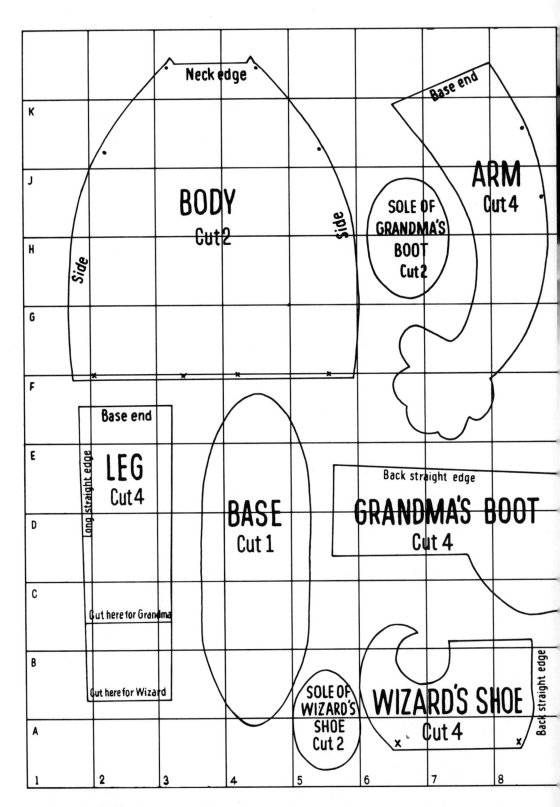

16-2   Basic Doll #2

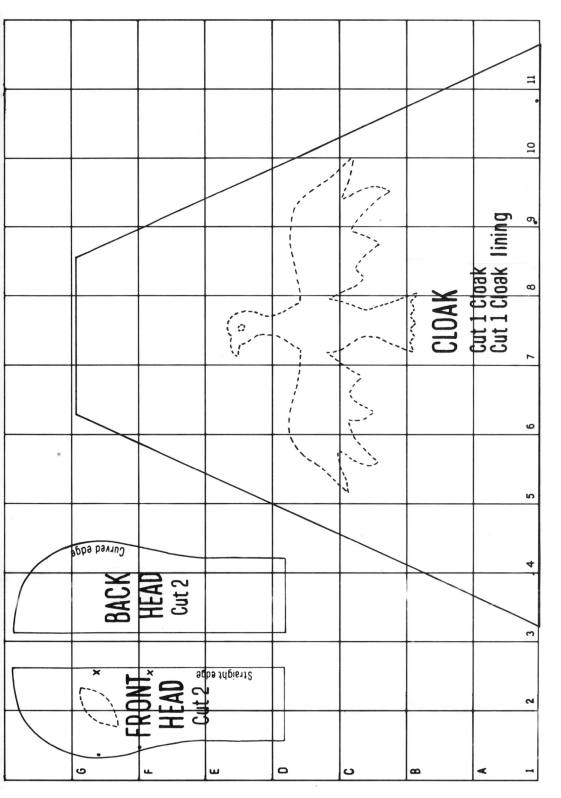

16-3 First part of pattern for Wendall

157

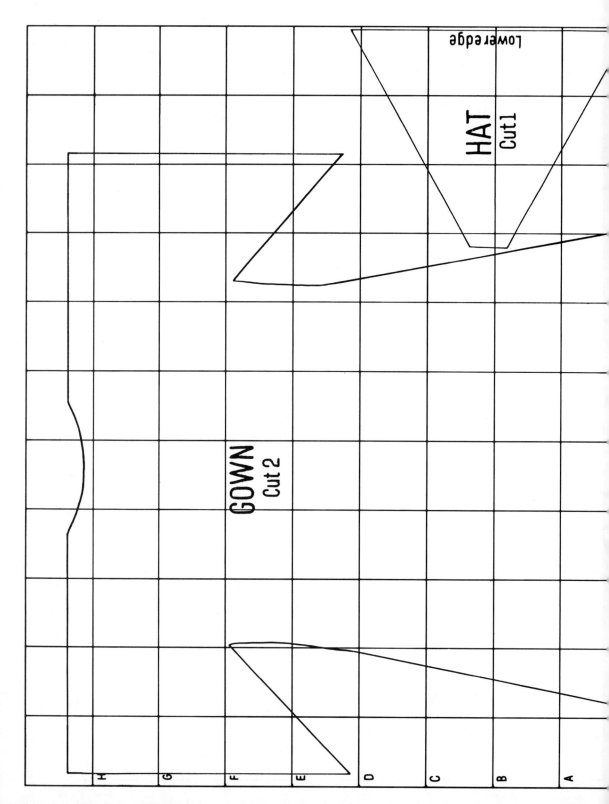

16-4   Second part of pattern for Wendall

158

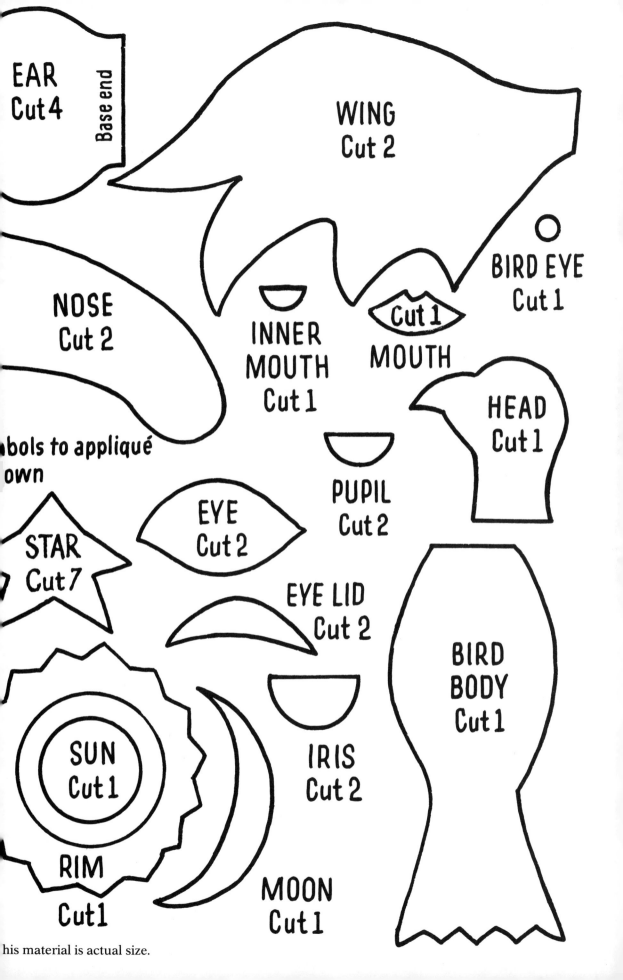

EAR
Cut 4

Base end

WING
Cut 2

BIRD EYE
Cut 1

NOSE
Cut 2

INNER
MOUTH
Cut 1

Cut 1

MOUTH

HEAD
Cut 1

bols to appliqué
own

PUPIL
Cut 2

STAR
Cut 7

EYE
Cut 2

EYE LID
Cut 2

BIRD
BODY
Cut 1

SUN
Cut 1

IRIS
Cut 2

RIM
Cut 1

MOON
Cut 1

his material is actual size.

extend ½ inch beyond the edge of the fabric and the tip should curve down toward the neck edge.

Stitch together the *straight* edge of the two *front* head pieces, stitching the nose between them as you proceed (Fig. 16-5a). Set this piece aside and stitch the *curved* edge of the two back head pieces together (Fig. 16-5b).

Stitch each pair of ear pieces together, leaving the base end open. Turn both ears right side out and press. Topstitch ¼ inch within the outer edge of each ear, but leave the base ends open. Pin an ear to each side of the front head piece between each pair of dots marked on the fabric (Fig. 16-5c). The base end of the ear should extend ¼ inch beyond the edge of the fabric. Baste the ears in place.

Stitch the front of the head to the back of the head (Fig. 16-5c), attaching the ears as you proceed. Trim the seams and trim the neck edge even. Turn the head right side out.

Stuff the head *firmly*. Turn ½ inch of fabric around the base of the neck to the inside. Cut an oval of fabric slightly larger than the neck opening and stitch it over the opening to keep the stuffing from escaping while you work on other parts of the toy.

There are four arm pieces, two for each arm. Stitch each pair together, but leave an opening between the two dots marked on the underside of each arm and leave the base end open. Turn the arms right side out.

Stitch together the *back straight* edge of two shoe pieces. Stitch together the *long straight* edge of two leg pieces. Press both pieces open and flat. Stitch the upper edge of the shoe to the lower edge of the leg (Fig. 15-5a). Close the assembled piece and stitch from the upper edge of the leg, down the front, and around to the point marked X on the bottom of the shoe. Stitch the second leg and shoe together. Turn both legs right side out.

Pin the arms to the right side of one body piece, between the dots marked on each side of the body piece (Fig. 10-6). The arms should curve upward toward the neck edge, and ¼ inch of the base end of the arm should extend beyond the edge of the fabric. Pin the legs to the lower edge of the body, between each pair of X's marked on the fabric (Fig. 10-6). The toes should point inward toward the body piece and ¼ inch of the base end of the leg should extend beyond the edge of the fabric.

With right sides together, align the second body piece over the first. Baste and then stitch the side seams of the two pieces, from the notch at the neck edge to the base of the piece, catching in the arms as you proceed. Baste the base to the lower edge of the front and back body pieces (Fig. 16-6a). Trim the base if necessary, but maintain an even curve or the doll will be lopsided. Stitch the base to the body: the legs will be stitched between the base and the front body piece at the same time. Turn the body right side out through the opening between the two notches.

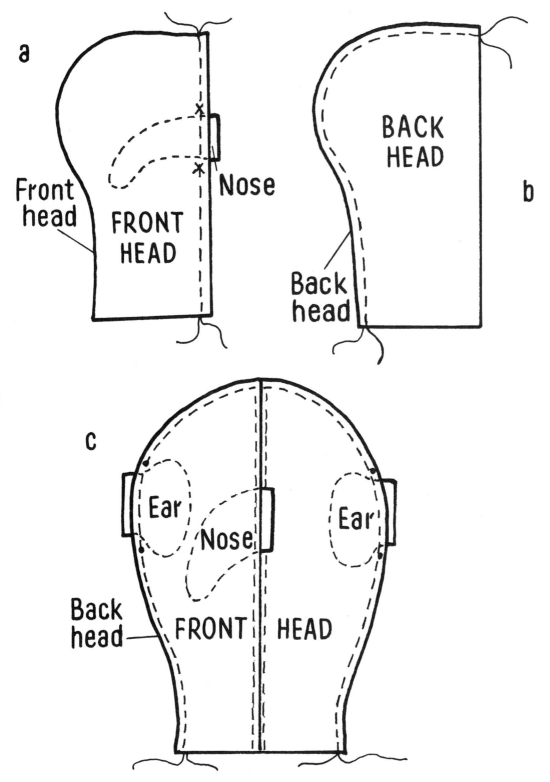

16-5a. Stitching together the two front head pieces, catching in the nose
   b. Stitching together the curved edge of the two back head pieces
   c. Stitching the front of the head to the back of the head, catching in the ears

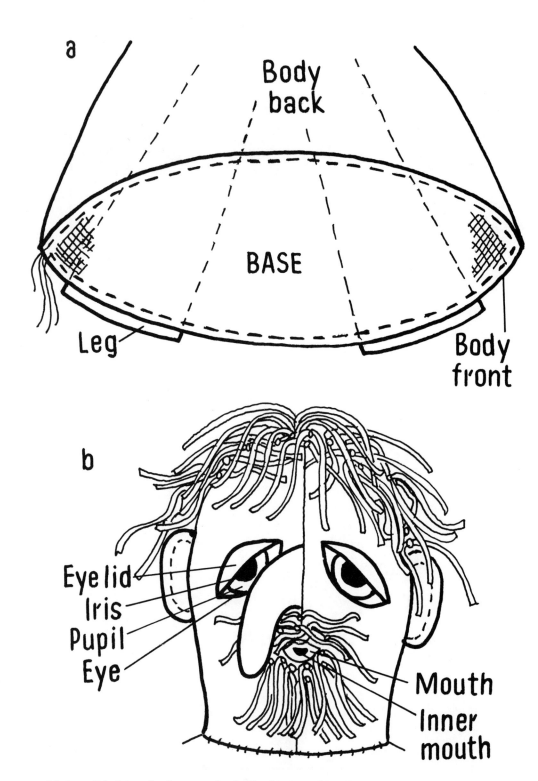

a

Body
back

BASE

Leg

Body
front

b

Eye lid
Iris
Pupil
Eye

Mouth
Inner
mouth

16-6a. Stitching the base to the body front and back, catching in the legs
    b. Positioning the features on the face

162 Wendall Wizard

Turn ¼ inch of fabric to the inside, around the edge of the opening in the base of the shoe. Stitch a sole over the opening, turning the raw edges of the sole to the inside as you proceed. Stop stitching when a 1-inch wide opening remains between the shoe and the sole. Stuff the leg and shoe *moderately firm,* pushing the stuffing through the 1-inch opening. Finish stitching the sole to the shoe, then repeat and stitch the second sole to the shoe, then stuff the second leg.

Stuff each hand and arm through the opening in the lower arm. Stuff the arms so that they are rounded out, but not bulging. Stitch the opening in the underarms shut, turning ¼ inch of fabric along the raw edges to the inside as you do so.

Stuff the body, but leave a gap in the stuffing at the neck so that there is room to insert the neck. Turn ¼ inch of fabric around the neck edge to the inside. Insert the neck. Stitch the fabric of the neck securely to the neck edge.

STEP THREE

At this point, Wendall looks rather strange with his long limbs, fat body, egg-shaped head, pointed nose, and large ears. But hair and features will make a great difference in his appearance, changing him from a grotesque looking creature to a dignified old wizard.

Wendall's hair should cover the crown of his head. Thread a sharp large-eyed needle with a 6-inch strand of mohair yarn. Stitch the yarn through the head fabric, just in front of the upper edge of one ear. There should be half a strand of yarn on each side of the point where the needle penetrates the fabric. Remove the needle and tie the strand in a secure knot (Fig. 15-6). Continue stitching strands of yarn just in front of the seamline that runs between the two ears, keeping the strands close together. End the row just in front of the upper edge of the second ear. Turn Wendall over and stitch a row of yarn in a straight line across the back of his head, level with the middle of his ears. Fill in the area between the two rows of yarn with knotted strands of yarn.

Refer to Fig. 16-6b, illustrating the way features are placed on the wizard's face. Glue the pupil to the eye, the iris to the pupil, and the lid over both. Then glue an assembled eye to each side of the head, over the ovals marked on the fabric for placement. Next glue the center mouth piece to the main mouth piece, then glue the assembled mouth to the head, about ¾ inch below the nose. When the glue has dried, stitch the features to the fabric by hand with clear nylon thread.

For a mustache, stitch a line of 3-inch long strands of yarn between the nose and the mouth. The line should extend 1½ inches on each side of the nose and curve down toward the edges of the mouth. For Wendall's beard, stitch and knot the yarn the same way you did for the hair. Stitch three rows of yarn below his mouth.

STEP FOUR

Note: ¼-inch seams allowed.

Wendall's clothes are appliquéd with a variety of magical symbols. I have included patterns for some, but you can design more intricate ones of your own to add an elaborate touch.

For Wendall's underpants, press under ¼ inch on each *long* straight edge of the 9 × 20-inch splashy fabric. Stitch each pressed edge in place. Press another ¼ inch of fabric along one of these long edges to the inside, and zigzag stitch the edge in place by machine or hem it by hand. To form a casing for the elastic, turn 1½ inches of fabric to the inside along the opposite edge, press and stitch close to both edges of this piece. Thread a 12-inch length of 1-inch wide elastic through the casing, then stitch it to both ends of the casing. Stitch the narrow ends of the rectangle together. Trim the seam. Turn the underpants right side out and press. Put them on Wendall with the elastic around his waist; then with several hand stitches, stitch them together between his legs to simulate a crotch seam.

Cut a 2-inch slit from the neck edge down the center back of *one* gown piece: this is the back piece. Now lay the *front* piece flat on your work surface with the *right* side facing up and arrange the felt symbols of the moon, stars, and sun in a pattern you find pleasing. Next glue the symbols to the fabric with latex or cloth glue; and when the glue has dried, machine appliqué the pieces to the gown or stitch them down by hand with clear nylon thread.

Stitch the front of the gown to the back of the gown at the shoulder seams (Fig. 17-3). Stitch from the neck edge to the ends of the sleeves. Turn ¼ inch of fabric to the inside, around the neck edge and around the edges of the slash. Stitch this edge in place by hand or with a decorative machine stitch. Hem the ends of each sleeve in the same way. Stitch the underarm seams from the lower edge of the gown to the ends of the sleeves. Narrowly hem the base of the gown. Stitch a snap closure to the upper edge of the back slash opening. Turn the gown right side out and press. Put the gown on the doll.

Stitch a piece of bright yarn through the pointed tip of one of Wendall's shoes. Curl up the tip and stitch the same piece of yarn through the body of the shoe. Draw the yarn up tight to hold the tip of the shoe in place. Tie the yarn in a knot and then a bow. Sew a bell securely to his shoe beside the yarn bow. Repeat, curling over the top and stitching a bell to the second shoe.

Lay the piece of Wendall's cloak, with the markings for placement of the bird appliqué, right side up on your work surface. Then place the felt pieces of the bird appliqué on the cloak, following the dotted lines marked there. Glue the bird to the fabric; and when the glue has dried, machine appliqué or hand stitch it to the fabric.

With right sides together, stitch the cloak lining to the cloak, but leave an opening between the two dots marked on the fabric. Turn the piece right side out and press. Press ¼ inch of fabric along the edges of the opening to the inside. Topstitch close to the edge of the piece, sewing the edges of the opening shut as you proceed. Turn 1½ inches of the upper edge of the cloak to the *outside*, so that the lining is exposed. Now stitch close to the edge opposite the fold, forming a casing through which to thread the ribbon. Thread a 24-inch length of 1-inch wide ribbon through the casing. Tie the ribbon around the doll's neck, gathering up the neckline of the cloak.

Narrowly hem the wide lower edge of the triangular piece of fabric for the wizard's hat. With right sides together, stitch together the two long sides of the triangle to form a cone. Turn the cone right side out, then stuff it so that it will keep its shape. Stitch the hat to the crown of Wendall's head.

Wendall Wizard is ready to test the power of his magic over the hearts of children everywhere.

Chapter 17

Grandma Sally

A child should always say what's true
And speak when he is spoken to,
And behave mannerly at table;
At least as far as he is able.

Whole Duty of Children
Robert Louis Stevenson

GRANDMOTHERS can no longer be characterized as lumpy, white-haired women best known for their cooking. Grandmothers today are younger looking and more active in every field. But grandmothers are still particularly loved by their grandchildren, for who else gives them presents and cookies and kisses and yet rarely finds a reason to scold or spank them. Grandma Sally, however, is an old-fashioned type lady who bakes sugar cookies and is a repository of advice. She is 26 inches tall, has a broad, huggable body cut from pink, pale orange, or pale yellow medium-weight cotton. Her high-button boots are cut from navy blue brushed denim, but any number of other fabrics will simulate their texture. Her dress is a subdued, old-fashioned print cotton, but a patchwork or calico fabric makes a nice substitution. Her hair is grey Orlon yarn and her features are felt.

17-1 Grandma Sally

MATERIALS

1 yard of medium-weight cotton fabric for the body, head, arms, legs, base, ears, and nose.

¼ yard of a suitable fabric for the high-button shoes and soles of the shoes.

1 yard of white cotton flannel to line the doll.

½ yard of an old-fashioned print cotton for the dress.

¼ yard of fabric for the apron.

A 14-inch length of 1-inch wide lace to edge the apron, a 20-inch length of the same lace to edge the panties, and an 11½-inch length of ¾-inch wide lace for the collar.

A rectangle of fabric 9 × 20 inches for the panties.

A 2-ounce skein of grey Orlon yarn for the hair.

Scraps of felt in various colors for the features and the eyeglasses.

A yard of 1-inch wide satin ribbon for the apron waistband.

8 flat shiny buttons with ½-inch diameters and loops at the back for attaching them to fabric for the shoes.

A snap closure for the dress.

Thread to match fabric and clear nylon thread.

Kapok or Dacron to stuff the doll.

STEP ONE

Enlarge the patterns for the Basic Doll # 2 (Fig. 16-2) and for Grandma and her clothes (Fig. 17-2). From the fabrics you have chosen, cut the appropriate number of pieces as marked on the patterns. Transfer the markings for the features to the *right* side of the head fabric. Transfer all other markings to the *wrong* side of the fabric.

Cut lining pieces for all parts of the doll body, including the shoes, but not the soles. Pin the lining to the *wrong* side of each corresponding piece of fabric.

STEP TWO

Note: ¼-inch seams allowed. Unless otherwise stated, stitch with *right* sides together. Remove all pins before turning assembled pieces right side out.

Begin by assembling Grandma Sally's head. First stitch the two pieces of the nose together, leaving the base of the nose open. Turn the piece right side out and pad it *lightly* with stuffing, but leave 1 inch at the open

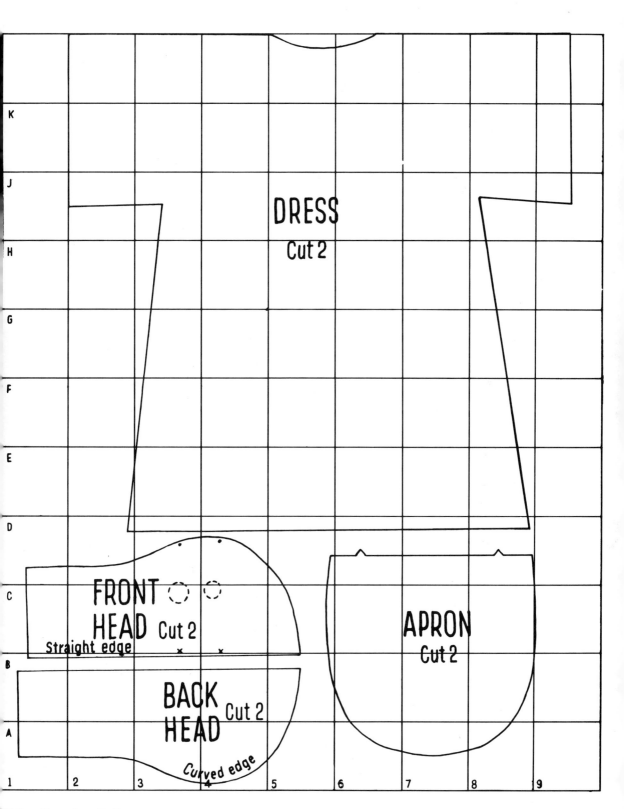

DRESS
Cut 2

FRONT
HEAD Cut 2
Straight edge

BACK
HEAD Cut 2
Curved edge

APRON
Cut 2

7-2 Grandma Sally

169

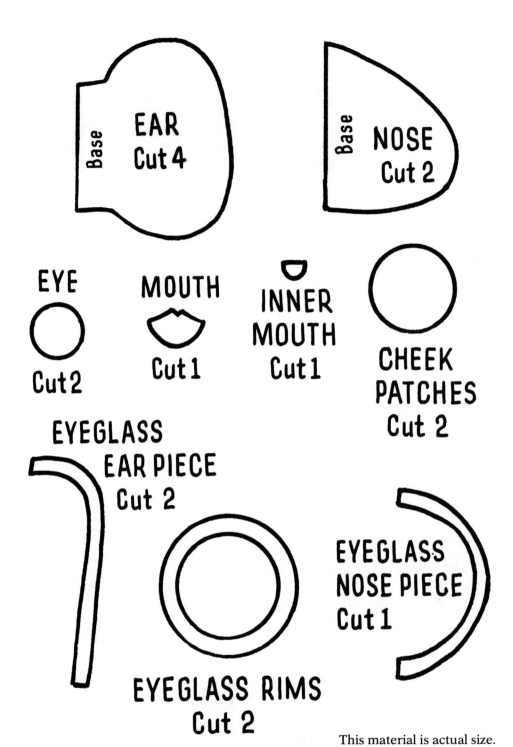

EAR
Cut 4

Base

NOSE
Cut 2

Base

EYE
Cut 2

MOUTH
Cut 1

INNER
MOUTH
Cut 1

CHEEK
PATCHES
Cut 2

EYEGLASS
EAR PIECE
Cut 2

EYEGLASS
NOSE PIECE
Cut 1

EYEGLASS RIMS
Cut 2

This material is actual size.

170

end unstuffed. Pin the nose to the right side of one head piece, positioning it between the two X's marked on the fabric (Fig. 16-5a). The base of the nose should extend ½ inch beyond the edge of the fabric.

Stitch the *straight* edge of the *front* head pieces together, stitching the nose between them as you proceed. Stitch the *curved* edge of the two back head pieces together (Fig. 16-5b).

Stitch each pair of ear pieces together, but leave the base of each ear open. Turn the ears right side out and press. Topstitch each ear, placing a row of stitching ¼ inch within the outer edge, but leave the base open. Pin an ear between each pair of dots marked on the front head piece (Fig. 16-5c). The base of the ear should extend ¼ inch beyond the edge of the fabric. Baste the ears to the head piece.

Stitch the front of the head to the back of the head (Fig. 16-5c), attaching the ears as you proceed. Trim the seam and trim the neck edge even. Turn the head right side out.

Stuff Grandma's head *firmly*. Turn ½ inch of fabric around the neck edge to the inside. Cut an oval of fabric ½ inch larger than the neck opening. Then stitch this piece over the opening, turning the raw edge to the inside as you proceed. This prevents the stuffing from escaping when you are working on other parts of the toy.

There are four arm pieces, two for each arm. Stitch each pair together, but leave an opening between the two dots marked on the underside of each arm and also leave the base of each arm open. Turn the arms right side out.

There are four pieces for Grandma's high-button shoes, two pieces for each shoe. Stitch together the *back straight* edge of each pair.

There are four leg pieces, two for each leg. Stitch *one* long straight edge of each pair together. Press the leg and the shoe assemblies open and flat, then stitch the upper edge of one shoe to the lower edge of one leg (Fig. 15-5a). Repeat for the second shoe and leg. Now close an assembled shoe and leg piece, and stitch from the upper edge of the leg, down the front, and around the shoe; but leave the base of the shoe open. Repeat for the second shoe and leg. Turn both pieces right side out.

Pin the arms to the right side of *one* body piece, between the dots marked on each side of the piece (Fig. 10-6). The arms should curve upward toward the neck and ¼ inch of the base of each arm should extend beyond the edge of the fabric. Pin the legs to the lower edge of the body, between each pair of X's marked on the lower edge of the fabric (Fig. 10-6). The toes should point inward toward the body and ¼ inch of the base of the leg should extend beyond the edge of the fabric.

Align the second body piece over the first, with right sides together. Baste and then stitch the side seams of the two pieces from the notch at the neck edge to the base of the piece, catching in the arms as you proceed. Baste the base to the lower edge of the front and back body piece (Fig. 16-6a). Trim the base for a correct fit. Stitch the base to the body, stitching the legs between the base and the body as you proceed. Turn the body right side out through the opening between the two notches.

Turn ¼ inch of fabric to the inside, around the edge of the opening in the base of one shoe. Stitch a sole over the opening, turning the raw edges of the sole to the inside as you proceed, leaving a 1-inch wide opening between the shoe and sole. Stuff the leg and shoe *moderately firm*, pushing the stuffing through the 1-inch opening. When you finish stuffing, stitch the 1-inch wide gap shut, then stitch around the perimeter of the sole once again for extra strength. Stitch and stuff the second leg.

Stuff each hand and arm through the openings in the underarms, stuffing until they are shapely and smooth but not lumpy. Stitch the openings in the underarms closed, turning ¼ inch of fabric along the raw edges to the inside as you stitch.

Stuff the body *moderately firm*, but leave a gap in the stuffing at the neck edge so that there is room to insert the neck. Turn ¼ inch of fabric around the neck edge to the inside. Insert the neck. Stitch the fabric of the neck securely to the neck edge.

STEP THREE

Now that Grandma's plump body is finished, it's time to add some hair to her head and set features to her face. Her hair is embroidered, much the same way as Tallulah Ballerina's, with a satin stitch (Figs. 3-3b and c). Choose a sharp needle with a large enough eye to thread Orlon yarn. Tie a knot at the end of a strand of yarn and embroider one side of the crown of the doll's head, then embroider the other side. The hair should run across the forehead, extending along and just behind the ear-to-ear seam. It should also run over the top of the head to about halfway between the crown of the head and the nape of the neck. Leave a narrow strip of fabric visible in the middle of the head to simulate a part in the hair.

For a row of bangs, cut a dozen pieces of 3-inch long strands of yarn, then stitch them along the ear-to-ear seam, pulling each strand halfway through the fabric so there is an equal amount of yarn on each side of the point where the needle penetrates the fabric. Remove the needle and tie the yarn in a knot. Stitch the entire row in this manner, then brush the yarn down over Grandma's forehead and trim the pieces into neat, short bangs.

For the old-fashioned bun on top of Grandma's head, first cut six 20-inch lengths of yarn. Stitch one length through the center top of the doll's head. Leave an equal length of yarn on each side of the point where the needle penetrates the fabric. Remove the needle and knot the yarn. Stitch and knot the five remaining lengths of yarn in a group that closely surrounds the original strand. You should now have twelve strands of yarn, each 10-inches long. Gather the yarn into three groups of four strands each and braid them, tying a strand of yarn around the end of the braid to hold it together. Twist the braid into a tight bun and stitch it to the top of the doll's head.

Glue the felt circles for Grandma Sally's eyes over the circles marked with dotted lines on the head fabric. Glue the cheek patches over the circles marked below the eyes. Glue the larger mouth piece ½ inch below the nose, then glue the center mouth piece to it. Glue the nose band for the glasses over Grandma's nose and glue the circles for the rims of the glasses around the eyes, overlapping the noseband. Before the rims dry, glue the eyeglass earpieces over Grandma's ears and slip the ends of the earpieces under the outside edge of the rims. After the glue has thoroughly dried, stitch the features and the eyeglasses to the fabric with clear nylon thread.

Stitch four buttons in a row, ½ inch apart from each other, to the ankles of the high-button shoes. Stitch the buttons *securely* to the fabric so they can not be pried loose.

STEP FOUR

Note: ¼-inch seams allowed.

Grandma Sally wears ruffled panties, a print dress, and a lacy apron. As an extra touch, you can knit or crochet an 8 × 20-inch shawl.

To make Grandma's panties, press under ¼ inch of fabric along each *long straight* edge of the 9 × 20-inch rectangle. Stitch both pressed edges in place. Stitch a 20-inch length of 1-inch wide lace edging to one of the stitched edges. Fold over and press an additional 1½ inches to the inside, along the opposite stitched edge. To form a casing for the elastic, stitch close to both edges of the pressed piece. Thread a 12-inch length of 1-inch wide elastic through the casing, then stitch the elastic to both ends of the casing. Stitch the narrow ends of the rectangle together. Put the panties on Grandma with the elastic around her waist and the lace around her legs. Stitch the panties together between her legs with a few hand stitches.

For Grandma's dress, first cut a 2-inch slit from the neck edge down the center back of *one* dress piece, this piece will be the back of the dress. Now stitch the front dress piece to the back dress piece at the shoulder seams, stitching from the neck edge to the ends of the sleeves (Fig. 17-3). Press ¼ inch of fabric to the inside around the neck edge and the edges of the slash. Stitch the pressed edge in place. For the collar, stitch the 11½-inch length of ¾-inch wide lace edging to the right side of the dress neck

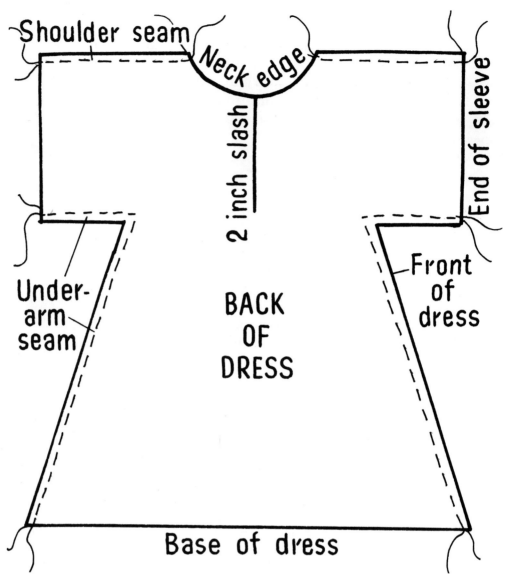

Shoulder seam

Neck edge

2 inch slash

End of sleeve

Under-
arm
seam

BACK
OF
DRESS

Front
of
dress

Base of dress

17-3   Stitching the back of the dress to the front of the dress

edge, turning ¼ inch of lace to the inside at the edges of the slash as you proceed. Hem the ends of the sleeves. Stitch together the underarm seams of the dress. By hand, stitch a snap closure to the neck edge of the slash. Try the dress on the doll and pin up a suitable hem. Take the dress off and hem by hand. Press the dress and put it back on the doll.

With the right sides of the fabric together, stitch around the perimeter of the two apron pieces, but leave the notched edge unstitched (Fig. 17-4a). Trim the seam to ⅛ inch. Turn the apron right side out and press, folding under ¼ inch of fabric along each of the notched edges. Stitch the 14-inch length of 1-inch wide lace to the curved edge of the apron (Fig. 17-4b).

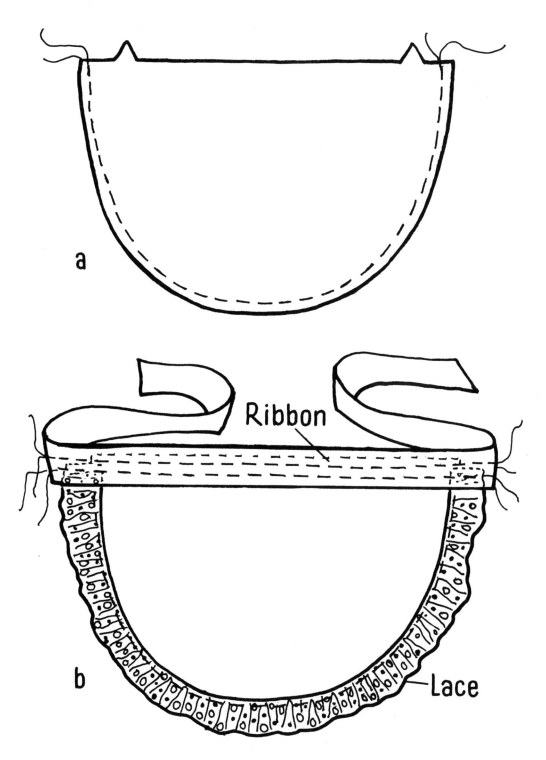

17-4a. Stitching together the two pieces of the apron
b. Stitching the lace and ribbon to the apron

Next fold the satin ribbon for the apron waistband in half and mark the halfway point on the wrong side of the ribbon with a pin. Now pin the wrong side of the ribbon to the right side of the notched edge of the apron, with the halfway point of the ribbon at the center front of the apron. The upper edge of the ribbon should be ⅛ inch beyond the upper edge of the apron fabric. Stitch the ribbon to the apron, placing two rows of stitching ¼ inch apart with the first row ¼ inch within the upper edge of the ribbon. Stitch together the open edges of the apron as you proceed (Fig. 17-4b). Put the apron on Grandma and tie the ribbon in a bow at the back.

Grandma Sally is now complete and ready to play with her favorite children.

Chapter 18

Baby Karen

Sleep, baby, sleep!
Thy father watches the sheep.
Thy mother is shaking the dreamland tree.
And down falls a little dream on thee.
Sleep, baby, sleep!

Sleep, Baby, Sleep
Old Lullaby

*B*ELIEVE it or not, the baby doll was a latecomer to the world of dolls, not appearing until the 1820s. Most dolls up to that time were miniature adults, all dressed in adult clothing. Children too, until the mid-nineteenth century, were dressed like adults and were expected to act grown up. However, once baby dolls were introduced, they were an astounding and lasting success, all but replacing most other dolls on the market.

Baby Karen is one of my favorite dolls. She is 16 inches long, soft and cuddly. She makes an excellent first doll for a little girl. If you stuff her with Dacron, she will be washable. You can make her from most any color fabric and can paint her eyes in whatever color of acrylic you choose. As you probably know, it's very difficult to buy a brown-eyed doll. The gown and bonnet are cut from a matching print cotton flannel and both are edged with lace. She wears a cotton diaper and booties made of a textured knit. Her neck and sleeve edges are bound with seam binding.

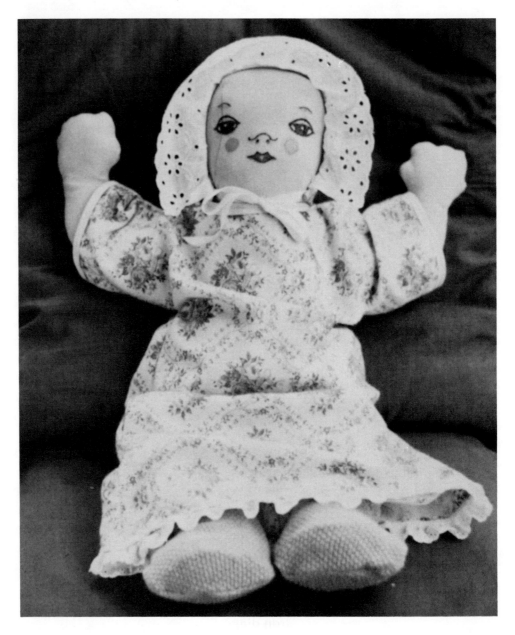

18-1 Baby Karen

178

MATERIALS

½ yard of medium-weight cotton for the body, head, gusset, arms, legs, and soles of the feet.

½ yard of white cotton flannel to line the doll.

⅓ yard of delicate printed cotton flannel for the gown, the bonnet, and the bonnet strip.

¼ yard of textured knit fabric of a pastel color for the booties.

An 8½-inch square of soft, white cotton fabric for the diaper.

1 yard of ¼-inch wide white satin ribbon for the bonnet ties and the ties at the dress neck edge.

A 21-inch length of ½-inch wide lace edging to trim the lower edge of the gown.

A 12-inch length of 2-inch wide white lace edging for the brim of the bonnet.

1 yard of ½-inch wide single fold bias tape to bind the edges of the neck and the sleeves of the gown.

Kapok or Dacron to stuff the doll.

Thread to match the fabric.

STEP ONE

Enlarge the patterns for Baby Karen and her clothes (Figs. 18-2 and 18-3). From the fabrics you have chosen, cut the appropriate number of pieces as marked on the patterns. Transfer all markings to the wrong side of the fabric.

Cut lining pieces from white cotton flannel for all parts of the doll body, except the soles of the feet. Do not cut lining pieces for her clothes. Pin the lining to the wrong side of each corresponding piece.

STEP TWO

Note: ¼-inch seams allowed. Unless otherwise stated, stitch fabric with *right* sides together. Remove all pins when turning assembled pieces right side out.

Begin with Baby Karen's head. First align the dot marked on the gusset with the dot marked on the head piece (Fig. 18-4a). Now baste the gusset to the side of the head, matching the curves. End the basting at the base of the back of the head, opposite the dot, and stitch. Align the X on the opposite side of the gusset with the dot marked on the second head piece. From this point, baste and then stitch the gusset to the head, again matching curves and ending the stitching at the base of the back of the head. Trim the seams to ⅛ inch. Turn the head right side out.

Firmly stuff the head, thoroughly filling out the curves of face and

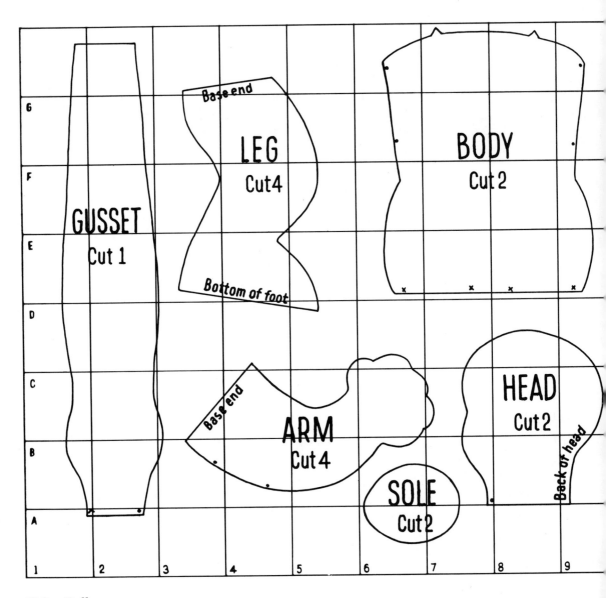

18-2   Doll

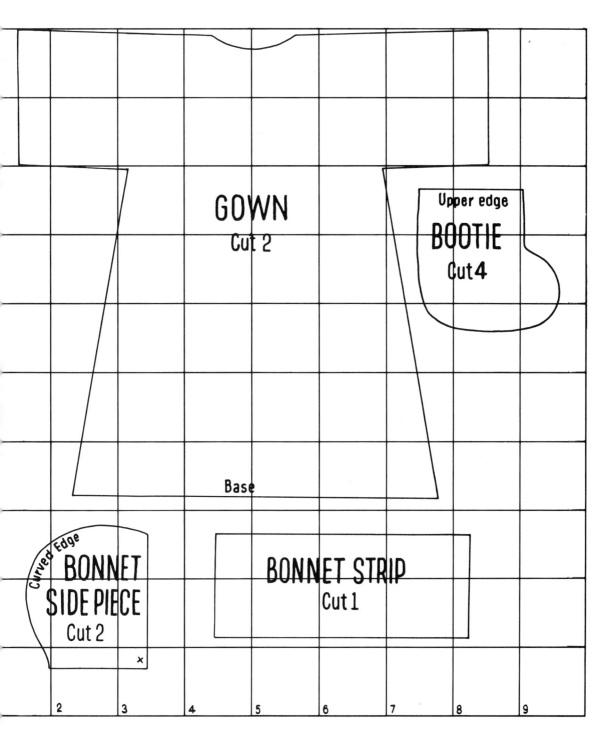

GOWN
Cut 2

Base

Upper edge
BOOTIE
Cut 4

Curved Edge
BONNET
SIDE PIECE
Cut 2

BONNET STRIP
Cut 1

2 3 4 5 6 7 8 9

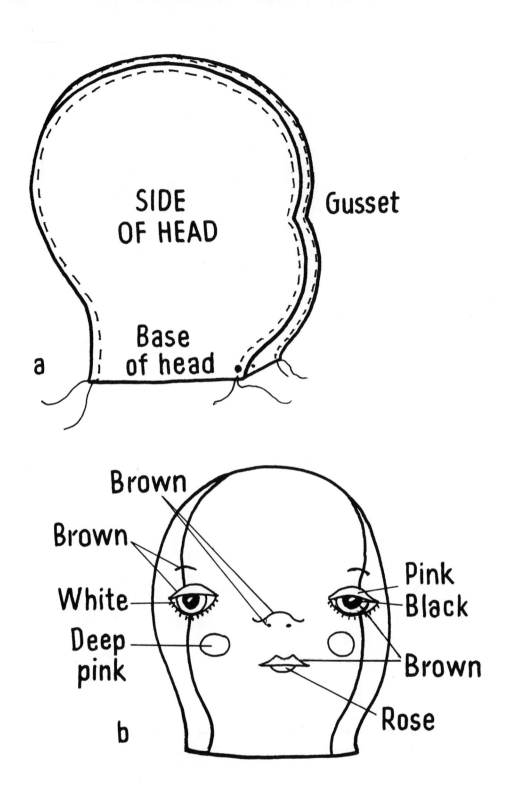

SIDE
OF HEAD

Gusset

Base
of head

a

Brown

Brown

White

Deep
pink

Pink
Black

Brown

Rose

b

18-4a. Stitching the gusset to the head
   b. Color guide for painting the features

cheeks. Turn ¼ inch of fabric around the neck edge to the inside. Cut an oval scrap of fabric ½ inch larger than the diameter of the neck opening. Stitch this piece over the opening, turning the raw edges to the inside as you proceed. Set the head aside.

There are four arm pieces, two for each arm. Stitch each pair together, but leave an opening between the dots marked on the underside of each arm and also leave the base of the arms open. Turn the arms right side out.

There are four leg pieces, two for each leg. Stitch the side seams of each pair of legs together, leaving the bottom of the foot unstitched and the base of the leg open. Turn the legs right side out.

Pin the arms to the right side of one body piece. Pin an arm between each pair of dots marked on the fabric (Fig. 10-6). The arms should curve upward toward the neck edge. At the base end of the arm, ¼ inch should extend beyond the edge of the body fabric. Pin the legs to the lower edge of the body piece between each pair of X's marked on the fabric. The base end of the leg should extend ¼ inch beyond the edge of the fabric and the toes should point inward toward the body piece.

With right sides together, align the second body piece with the body piece to which the limbs are pinned. Stitch the shoulder seams of the two pieces together from the notch marked at the neck edge to the edge of the fabric. Stitch together the side seams of the two pieces. Stitch the base of the two pieces together. Trim the seams. Turn the body right side out.

Turn ¼ inch of fabric around the base of one foot to the inside. Stitch the sole to the foot, turning the raw edges of the sole to the inside as you proceed. Leave 1 inch of sole open and then stuff the leg through this opening. Stuff *loosely*, filling out the shape of the leg, but keeping the joint where the leg attaches to the body extremely *flexible*. When you finish stuffing the leg, stitch the 1-inch opening between the sole and foot. Stitch around the perimeter of the sole once again. Repeat and stitch the sole to the second foot, then stuff the leg.

Stuff the hands and the arms through the openings in the underside of the arms. Fill out the shape of the arms, but keep the stuffing loose at the joints where the arms attach to the body, keeping the joints flexible. When you finish stuffing, turn ¼ inch of fabric to the inside, around the edges of the underarm openings, and stitch.

Stuff the body, filling out the form but leaving it soft and squeezable. Turn ¼ inch of fabric to the inside around the neck edge. Insert the neck into the opening. Stitch the neck securely to the fabric at the neck edge.

STEP THREE

Look carefully at Fig. 18-4b, the color guide for Baby Karen's features. The colors given are suitable for a pink head. Follow the design and draw the features very lightly on the fabric with a pencil. Be sure to keep the pencil marks light: if you make a mistake, a light mark can be erased with a gum eraser. After you make an accurate sketch of the face, paint the inside areas of the features with color, then paint the outlines in the darker colors. Use a nontoxic brand of acrylic paint. After it dries, coat the painted areas with acrylic gloss varnish. Don't varnish the unpainted areas.

STEP FOUR

Note: ¼-inch seams allowed.

Begin Baby Karen's clothing with her diaper. Narrowly hem all four edges of the diaper fabric. Put the diaper on the doll just as you would for a real baby. If the child who is getting the doll is old enough, hold the corners of the diaper together with small safety pins; if not, stitch the corners together.

The booties are next. Be sure the fabric has some give to it, because the booties need to stretch over the doll's feet. Stitch around the perimeter of each pair of bootie pieces, leaving the upper edges open. Trim the seams. Turn ¼-inch hem to the inside around the upper edge of each bootie and stitch the hem in place. Turn the booties right side out and put them on the doll.

The gown is made much the way you make one for a real baby. First take one of the gown pieces and cut a 2-inch slit from the neck edge down the center: this is the back gown piece. Now align the front gown piece with the back gown piece and stitch together the shoulder seams from the neck edge to the tips of the sleeves (Fig. 17-3).

The raw edges along the ends of the sleeves, the neck edge, and the slit are bound with seam binding, which gives a smooth, neat and decorative finish to the gown. This procedure is easier to illustrate than explain; so before you begin, look carefully at Fig. 18-5. First measure the length of the raw edge at the end of the sleeve to be bound, then cut a piece of bias tape this length *plus* ½ inch. Open out one folded edge of the tape and pin the *right* side of it to the *wrong* side of the sleeve. The raw edges of the tape should extend ¼ inch beyond the edge of the fabric on each side. The edge of the tape should be ⅛ inch within the edge of the sleeve. Stitch the tape of the sleeve, keeping your stitching ¼ inch inside the edge of the tape, along the fold line. Trim the sleeve even with the edge of the tape. Fold the tape to the outside, over the end of the sleeve. By hand and with small neat stitches, stitch the folded edge of the tape to the sleeve. Bind the second sleeve in the same manner. Bind the neck edge and the edges of the slash as one long piece, cutting 1 inch extra of the bias tape at the ends. Again, the raw ends of the tape should meet at the lower end of the slash, as above.

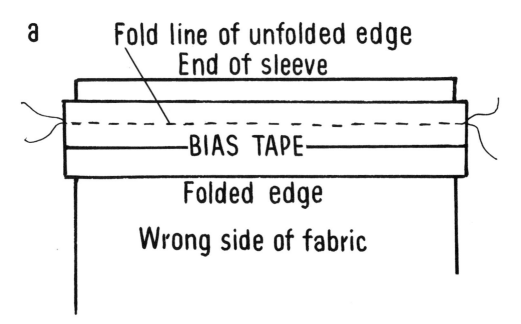

a

Fold line of unfolded edge
End of sleeve

BIAS TAPE

Folded edge

Wrong side of fabric

Bias tape folded over end of sleeve

Right side of fabric

b

18-5a. Stitching bias tape to the wrong side of the sleeve
  b. Folding bias tape over the end of the sleeve and stitching tape to the right side of the sleeve

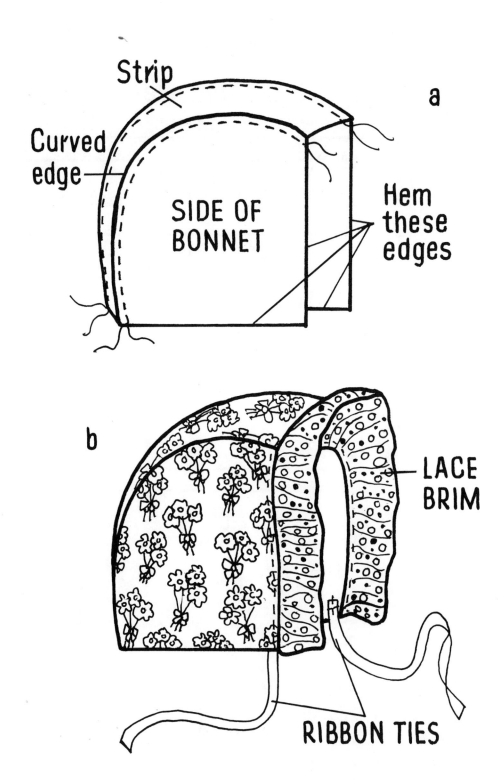

18-6a.   Stitching the strip to the side of the bonnet and hemming the raw edge
   b.   Stitching the lace brim and the ribbon ties to the bonnet

Stitch the underarm seams of the gown, from the ends of the sleeves to the lower edge of the gown.

Press ¼ inch of fabric around the base of the gown to the inside and stitch the pressed edge in place. Pin the 21-length of lace edging to the lower edge of the gown, with the ends of the piece meeting at the center back. Stitch the lace to the gown. Now stitch the ends of the lace together, keeping the seam on the inside of the gown. Cut two 8-inch lengths of ¼-inch wide white satin ribbon. Stitch the end of a ribbon to the inside of each of the edges of the slash at the neck edge. Turn the gown right side out. Press. Put the dress on the doll.

Last of all, make Karen's bonnet. First stitch the bonnet strip to one bonnet side piece, stitching the strip to the curved edge of the piece (Fig. 18-6a). Next stitch the curved edge of the second bonnet side piece to the opposite edge of the strip. Trim the seams. Hem all the raw edges of the assembled piece ¼ inch. To make the bonnet brim, stitch a 12-inch length of 2-inch wide lace edging to the inside front edge of the bonnet (Fig. 18-6b). To make the ties, stitch two 8-inch lengths of ¼-inch wide white satin ribbon to the inside of the lower front edges at each of the two points marked X. Put the bonnet on the doll and tie a bow under her chin.

Baby Karen is ready to play.

Chapter 19

Crawdon Crocodile

> How does the little crocodile
>   Improve his shining tail,
> And pour the waters of the Nile
>   On every golden scale!
>
> How cheerfully he seems to grin,
>   How neatly spreads his claws,
> And welcomes little fishes in,
>   With gently smiling jaws!
>
> *The Crocodile*
> Lewis Carroll

AMERICAN crocodiles and alligators were once common in Southern swamps but were hunted almost to extinction. Fortunately, conservation laws were enacted to protect them and they are making an amazing comeback. Crocodiles are smaller and of lighter build than alligators. They have a narrow, pointed snout with teeth protruding from the side. Crocodiles prefer salt water, while alligators like fresh water. Both eat fish, turtles, birds, and other water life. For all their grotesque reputations and fearsome appearances, most crocodiles will avoid men. Only certain crocodiles of the Nile and Southern Asia are known to attack humans.

Crawdon Crocodile is an ambiguous fellow. Although he wears a loud shirt, he is really very shy and would love to have a friend. His back, tail, arms, and legs are cut from a bright green flower-printed cotton. His belly can be cut from off-white no-wale, ribless corduroy; velvet; velveteen; or brushed denim. His eyes are made from two pairs of buttons sewn together. His nostrils are felt. His shirt is a splashy Hawaiian print cotton. He measures 22 inches long.

19-1   Crawdon Crocodile

MATERIALS

¾ yard of sturdy, printed cotton for the back, upper jaw, tail, arms, and legs.

⅓ yard of off-white fabric for the belly and lower jaw.

1 yard of cotton flannel to line the doll.

A 9 × 12-inch rectangle of felt for the hat.

Two large, flat buttons with 2-inch diameters for the eyes, and two smaller, flat black buttons with ½-inch diameters for the pupils.

Scraps of felt for the nostrils and inner nostrils.

1 yard of yarn to crochet a hatband.

Kapok or Dacron to stuff the doll.

Thread to match the fabric and clear nylon thread.

STEP ONE

Enlarge the patterns for Crawdon Crocodile and his clothes (Figs. 19-2, 19-3, and 19-4). From the fabrics you have chosen, cut the appropriate number of pieces as marked on the pattern. Transfer the X's for the eyes, the circles for the nostrils, and the stitching lines for fingers and toes to the *right* side of the upper jaw, arms, and legs. Transfer the dots and X's to the *right* side of the body front. Transfer all other markings to the *wrong* side of the fabric.

Cut lining pieces for the upper and lower jaws, the back and front body pieces, the arms, legs, and tail. Pin the lining to the *wrong* side of each corresponding piece.

STEP TWO

Note: ¼-inch seams allowed. Unlesss otherwise stated, stitch with right sides of fabric together. Remove all pins when turning assembled pieces right side out.

Begin by attaching the upper jaw to the back body piece. Both pieces have an *outward* curve. With right sides of the upper jaw and the back body piece together, match the outward curve and the notches on each piece. Baste the two pieces together between the two notches (Fig. 19-5a) and stitch them together, beginning at the first notch and stitching to the second notch.

Both the lower jaw and the front body piece have an *inward* curve on one end. With right sides of the fabric together, match this curve and the notches, then baste the pieces together between the notches (Fig. 19-5b). Stitch from the first notch to the second notch.

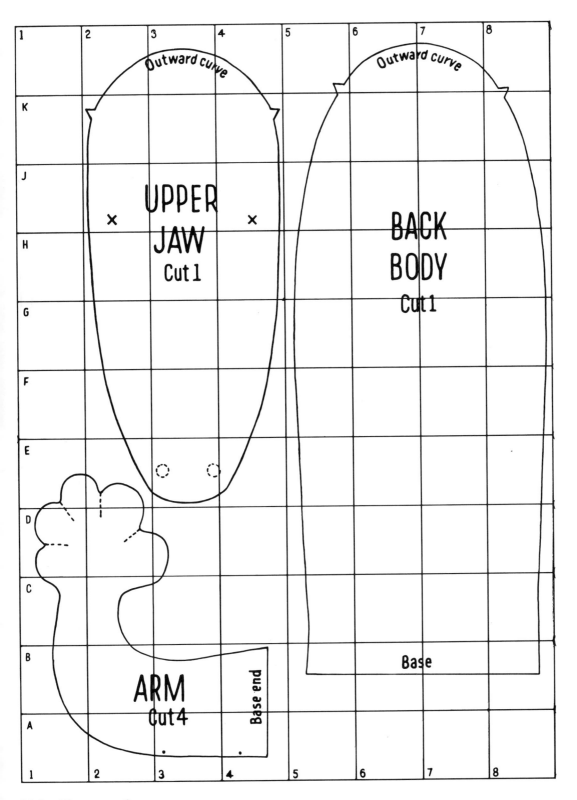

19-2   First part of pattern

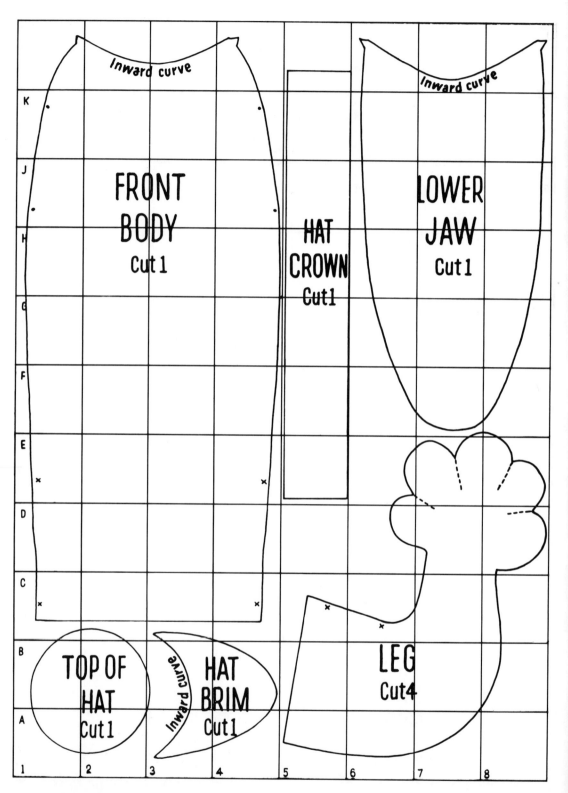

19-3   Second part of pattern

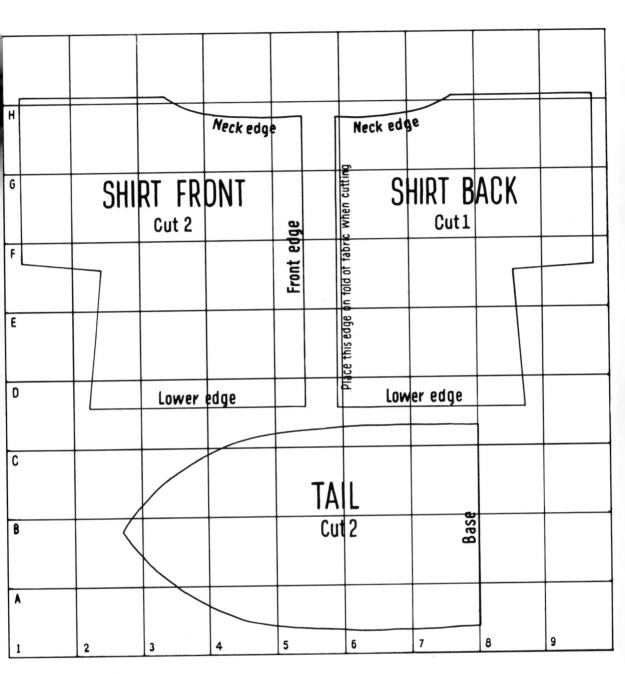

19-4   Last part of pattern

This material is actual size.

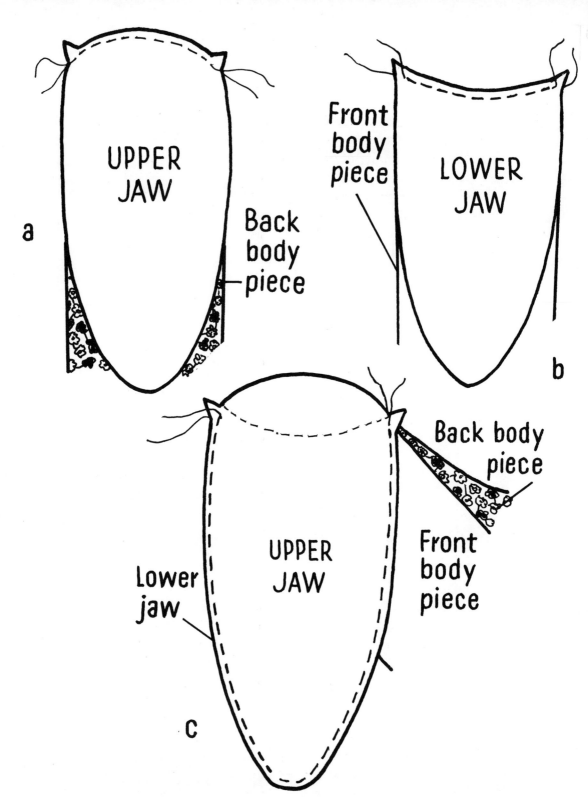

19-5a. Stitching the upper jaw to the back body piece
    b. Stitching the lower jaw to the front body piece
    c. Stitching the upper jaw to the lower jaw

With right sides of the fabric together, align the notches of the upper jaw with the notches of the lower jaw and baste the two pieces together. Stitch around the entire perimeter of the jaw, beginning at one set of notches and ending at the second set (Fig. 19-5c).

Stitch the two tail pieces together, but leave the base open. Turn the tail right side out. Fill the tail out *fully*, stuffing to within 1 inch of the open end. With right sides together, attach the base end of the tail to the base of the back body piece, also stitching the open end of the tail closed.

There are four arm pieces, two for each arm. Stitch each pair together, but leave the base end open and leave an opening between the two dots marked on the underside of the arm. Turn each arm right side out, then machine stitch along the dotted stitching lines marked on the hands. There are three lines of stitching on each hand. Stitching these lines also stitches the hand pieces together. When you push stuffing up between the stitching lines, it creates the illusion of fingers.

There are four leg pieces, two for each leg. Stitch each pair together, but leave an opening between the X's marked on the underside of each thigh and leave the base end open. Turn the legs right side out. To create the illusion of toes, stitch along the stitching lines marked on the feet.

Pin the arms to the *right* side of the body front, between each pair of dots marked on the fabric. The arms should curve upward toward the jaw. Fold and pin them in position so that, with the exception of the seamline, they will not interfere with stitching. The base end of the arm should extend ¼ inch beyond the seamline (Fig. 10-6). Pin the legs to the right side of the front body piece, between each pair of X's marked on the fabric. The legs should curve downward. These too should be folded and pinned to avoid interference with the stitching. The base should extend ¼ inch beyond the seamline.

With right sides together, attach the body front to the body back along the side seams, stitching each side seam from the point where the upper and lower jaws are joined to the base of the toy, catching in the arms and legs as you proceed.

Turn Crawdon right side out through the unstitched base. Stuff the jaw and the body *firmly*. Thoroughly fill out the curve of the jaw, then stuff the body. When you finish stuffing, turn ½ inch of fabric around the edges of the base opening to the inside. With clear nylon thread, stitch this opening securely closed.

Fill the arms and the legs through the openings in the underside of each, stuffing so that they are a little bit floppy, and not as firm as the body. Use a blunt instrument, like the eraser end of a pencil, to push tiny wads of stuffing between the stitching lines of the fingers and toes. As you finish each limb, turn ¼ inch of fabric around the edges of the opening to the inside, then stitch the opening closed.

STEP THREE

Crawdon has large, lumpy button eyes. First, for the pupils, stitch a small black button to the center of each of the larger buttons. Next stitch the larger button over each of the two X's marked on the upper jaw. Take special care that the buttons cannot be pried or chewed loose by a young child.

Use a cloth glue and glue a nostril over each of the two circles marked on the end of Crawdon's jaw, then glue the inner nostrils to the center of each nostril. When the glue has dried, attach the inner nostril to the outer nostril and stitch to the fabric. Here again, clear nylon thread works well to hide the stitching.

STEP FOUR

Note: ¼-inch seams allowed.

Crawdon has a short-sleeved shirt open at the throat. With right sides together, stitch one front shirt piece to the shirt back at the shoulder seam, stitching from the neck edge to the tip of the sleeve. Stitch the second front shirt piece to the shirt back at the shoulder seam, stitching from the neck edge to the tip of the sleeve. Now stitch both underarm seams from the underside of the sleeves to the lower edge of the shirt. If you have trouble determining where the shoulder seam or the underarm seam is located, refer to Fig. 17-3. To hem the neck edge, turn ¼ inch of fabric to the inside, press it in place and then stitch it down: a decorative stitch adds a nice touch to the hem. Now hem the sleeves and the lower edge of the shirt. Next turn ½ inch of fabric to the inside along the front open edges of the shirt. Press and stitch these edges in place. Turn the shirt right side out and press it before you put in on the doll.

To make Crawdon's hat, first overlap the two ends of the rectangular crown piece ½ inch and then glue the overlap together. Glue the circular top hat piece over one open end of the crown. Refer to the first two parts of Fig. 11-5a, illustrating the making of Cavalier Cat's hat, to see how the crown is glued together. Next glue the inward curve, opposite the pointed end of the brim, to the lower edge of the crown. Turn the hat upside down and prop the brim until the glue dries. The seam on the crown should be in the back, opposite the brim. After the glue has dried, stuff the crown of the hat so that it will hold its shape. Put the hat on Crawdon's head, positioning it over the bulge where the upper jaw is joined to the back body piece. Stitch the brim and hat securely to the head so that the stuffing cannot escape. Crochet a chain of yarn 13 inches long (Fig. 7-4b) and tie it around the crown of Crawdon's hat for a hatband.

Crawdon Crocodile is ready for an adventure.

Chapter 20

Cyrus Centaur

Playing upon the hill three centaurs were!
They lifted each a hoof! They stared at me
And stamped the dust!

The Centaurs
James Stephens

CENTAURS are mythological creatures with the head and torso of a man and the body, legs, and tail of a horse. Although some centaurs were aggressive and lustful, others were renowned musicians and teachers. The ancient Greeks were said to be very fond of horses, and therefore gave the centaur a complex nature. Cyrus Centaur is also complex. To make him, you will utilize most of the skills gained from the earlier dolls.

Cyrus, being half man, half horse, is cut from two different fabrics. His body and belly are no-wale or ribless corduroy of a rust color. His torso, head, and arms are cut from pale orange, medium-weight cotton. His hair and beard are fringe. His vest is cut from imitation fur fabric. He measures 22 inches.

20-1   Cyrus Centaur

MATERIALS

½ yard of fabric, such as no-wale corduroy, for the body, belly, gusset, and strip.

½ yard of medium-weight, flesh-colored fabric for the torso, head, nose, and arms.

1 yard of white cotton flannel to line the toy.

A 9 × 12-inch rectangle of black felt for the soles of the feet, and scraps of orange felt for cheek patches.

⅓ yard of imitation fur fabric for the vest.

A clean, empty plastic bottle to reinforce the soles of the feet.

A wire coat hanger for armatures.

2 yards of 1-inch wide brown cotton fringe for the hair and beard.

Embroidery thread in red, black, and white for the features.

Several yards of black rug yarn for the tail.

Thread to match the fabric and clear nylon thread.

Kapok or Dacron to stuff the toy.

STEP ONE

Enlarge the patterns for Cyrus Centaur and his vest (Figs. 20-2 and 20-3). From the fabrics you have chosen, cut the appropriate number of pieces as marked on the patterns. Transfer the markings for the features and the dots to the *right* side of the front head pieces. Transfer the stitching lines to the *right* sides of the hands. Transfer all other markings to the *wrong* side of the fabric.

From the white cotton flannel, cut pieces for lining the torso, head, nose, arms, body, belly, gusset, and strip. Pin the lining fabric to the *wrong* side of each corresponding piece.

Use the sole pattern as a guide and cut four sole reinforcements from the plastic bottle. Trim the perimeter of each sole ¼ inch.

STEP TWO

Note: ¼-inch seams allowed. Unless otherwise stated, stitch fabric with *right* sides together. Remove all pins when turning assembled pieces right side out.

Cyrus' horse-like body and his human torso and head are assembled and stuffed separately and then are stitched together.

Start by stitching the two nose pieces together, leaving the notched edge open. Turn the nose right side out and pad it with a tiny bit of stuffing.

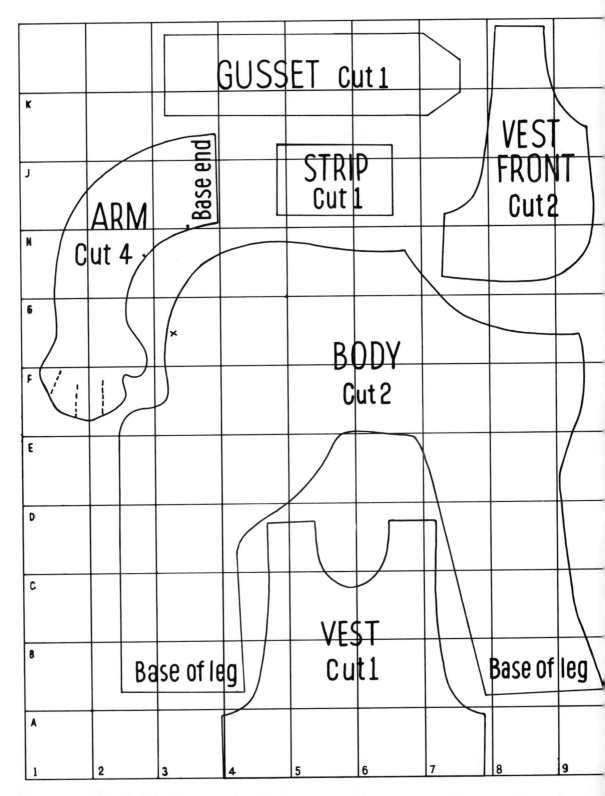

GUSSET Cut 1

STRIP Cut 1

VEST FRONT Cut 2

ARM Cut 4

Base end

BODY Cut 2

x

VEST Cut 1

Base of leg

Base of leg

20-2   First part of pattern

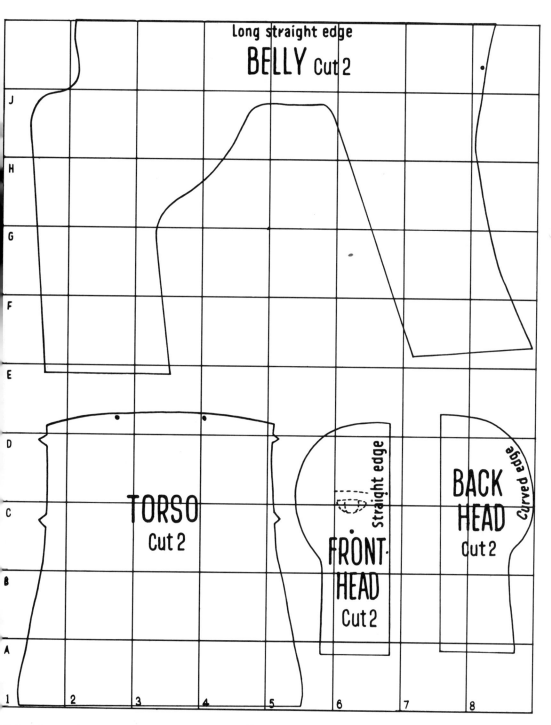

Long straight edge
BELLY Cut 2

J
H
G
F
E
D

TORSO
Cut 2

straight edge

FRONT HEAD
Cut 2

Curved edge

BACK HEAD
Cut 2

C
B
A
1   2   3   4   5   6   7   8

0-3   Second part of pattern

CHEEK PATCH

○

Cut 2

NOSE
Cut 2

This material is actual size.

201

Pin the nose to the *right* side of one head piece, positioning the notched edge of the nose between the two dots marked on the piece. The base of the nose should extend ¼ inch beyond the seamline. With right sides together, align the second head piece over the first. Stitch the straight edge of the two pieces together, catching in the nose as you proceed (Fig. 20-4a).

Stitch together the curved edge of the two back head pieces (Fig. 20-4a). With the right sides of the fabric together, stitch the front head piece to the back head piece (Fig. 20-4a). Turn the head right side out. *Firmly* stuff the head. Turn ¼ inch of fabric around the neck edge to the inside. Cut an oval of scrap fabric with a diameter ¼ inch larger than the opening. Stitch the oval over the opening, turning the raw edges to the inside as you proceed. Set the head aside.

There are four arm pieces, two for each arm. Stitch each pair together, but leave the base end open and leave an opening between the dots marked on the underarm. Turn the arms right side out. Topstitch along each of the three stitching lines marked on each hand.

Pin the arms to the right side of one body piece, between the two notches. The arms should curve downward, toward the base of the torso. The base of each arm should extend ¼ inch beyond the seamline. Baste the arms to the torso (Fig. 20-4b).

With right sides of the fabric together, align the two torso pieces. Stitch together the side seams of the two pieces, catching in the arms as you do so. Stitch the shoulder seams from the dot marked at the neck to the shoulder edge.

Turn the torso right side out, then stuff it *firmly*. Leave enough of a gap in the stuffing at the neck opening so that there will be room to insert the neck. Turn ¼ inch of fabric around the base of the torso to the inside. Cut an oval of scrap fabric with a diameter ½ inch larger than the base opening. Stitch the oval over the opening, turning the raw edges of the piece to the inside as you proceed.

Turn ¼ inch of fabric around the torso neck opening to the inside. Insert the neck end of the head into the opening. Position the head so that it faces forward. Stitch the neck fabric securely to the fabric at the torso neck edge.

Stuff the arms through the openings in their under sides. Stuff them *moderately firm,* so they will hang freely and be movable. Stuffing between the finger stitching lines may be a little difficult. Use only a tiny amount of stuffing at a time, and push it between the stitching lines with the blunt end of a small crochet hook. Be careful not to rip the fabric. After you finish stuffing the fingers, the hands, and the arms, turn the edges of the underarm openings to the inside and stitch the openings shut. Set the torso assembly aside for the time being.

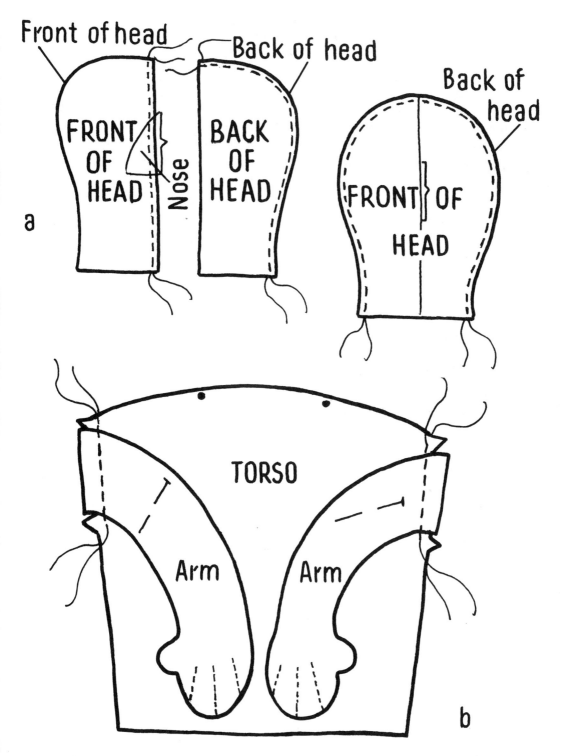

20-4a. Stitching together the pieces of the head
  b. Basting the arms to the torso

Now begin assembling the horse-like body of the doll. First, stitch together the *long straight* edge of the two belly pieces. Press the piece open and flat. Align the strip between the two dots marked on the belly piece, right sides of the fabric together (Fig. 6-3). Stitch the strip to the belly.

Align *one set* of front and rear legs of the *belly* piece with the front and rear legs of one *body* piece. Stitch the two pieces together from the X marked above the rear hind legs to the point where the strip is attached to the belly piece (Fig. 20-5). Leave the base of the legs open. Now stitch the strip to the chest. Next stitch the remaining set of front and rear legs to the second body piece, again starting to stitch at the X above the rear hind legs, leaving the base of the legs open and stitching the strip to the chest.

Baste one side of the gusset to each body piece. The tip of the gusset fits in the V formed by the two body pieces where they are attached to the belly piece at the X above the rear hind legs. Stitch the gusset to the body piece (Fig. 20-5). Turn the assembled piece right side out.

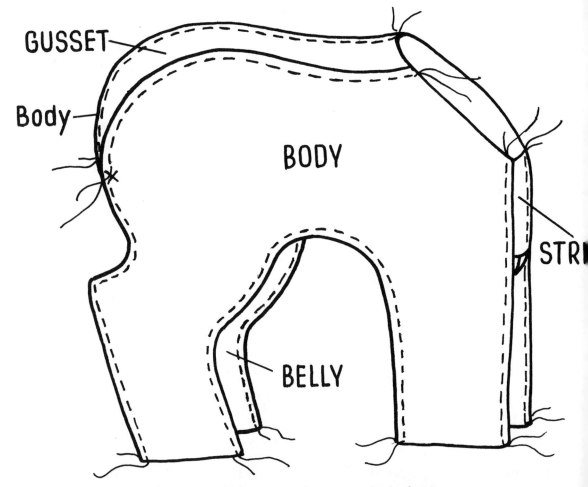

20-5   Attaching the belly strip and gusset to the body pieces

STEP THREE

Before you can stuff the horse-like body of the centaur, it is necessary to stitch a sole to the base of each leg. Turn ¼ inch of fabric around the base of one leg and insert a plastic sole into the opening. Place a black felt sole over the plastic. If either the plastic or the felt sole does not fit properly, trim it. Stitch the felt sole securely to the base of the leg (Fig. 6-6a). Repeat this procedure for the remaining three legs.

Now for the armatures. Cut the hook off a wire coat hanger, discard the hook, straighten out the remaining wire, and cut it in half so that you have two lengths each measuring approximately 16 inches. Bend each length into an arch (Fig. 7-4a). Turn 1 inch of wire on each end to form a loop. Wrap each loop with cloth tape so that no rough wire is left exposed to puncture the fabric. Insert one arch into the back legs of the horse body, with a loop in each hind leg. Insert the second arch into the front legs.

Firmly stuff the body of the doll, carefully concealing the armatures. Stuff the rear legs first, then the front legs. After the legs are stuffed, stuff above the rear hind legs, then the belly, and work forward to the opening.

Now the torso and the body assemblies are joined. First turn ¼ inch of fabric around the edges of the body assembly to the inside. About 1 inch of the torso assembly base should fit into the body assembly opening. To create a smooth juncture between the two assemblies, you will most likely have to remove or add stuffing. Insert the torso assembly into the body opening, then securely stitch the torso to the edge of the body opening, adding or removing stuffing to maintain a smooth body texture as you stitch.

STEP FOUR

To make Cyrus look more like a centaur, you have to attach his hair, beard, tail, and then embroider his features. Begin with the hair by cutting a 7-inch strip of fringe. Then stitch it along the seamline that joins the front to the back of the head (Fig. 20-6a). Stitch seven or eight strips of fringe behind the first, each piece ½ inch shorter than the piece preceding it.

The features are embroidered with stem and satin stitches, both illustrated in Fig. 3-3a and b. Use the stem stitch and black embroidery thread to stitch the eyebrows and to outline the eyes (Fig. 20-6b). Use the satin stitch and black embroidery thread to stitch in the pupils. Use the satin stitch and white embroidery thread to stitch the white of the eyes around the pupils. The centaur's mouth is positioned ⅛ inch below the nose. Use red embroidery thread and satin stitch an oval mouth ½ inch long and ⅛ inch wide. You may sketch the mouth on the fabric lightly in pencil before you begin stitching.

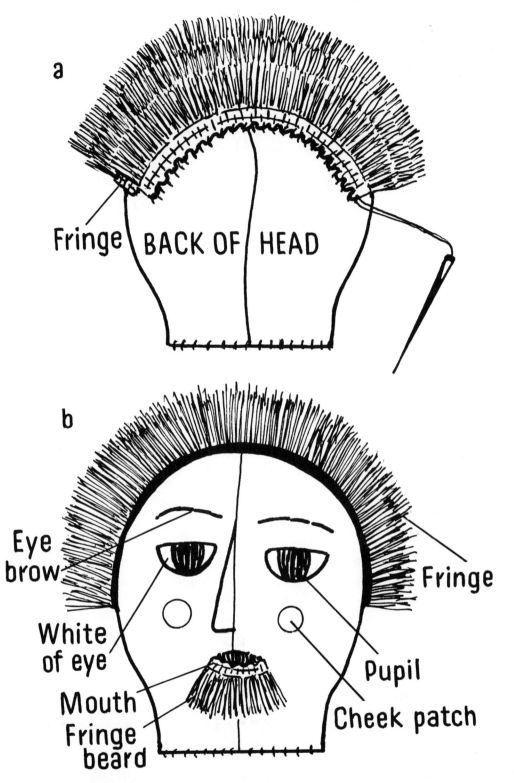

a

Fringe **BACK OF HEAD**

b

Eye brow

Fringe

White of eye

Pupil

Mouth
Fringe
beard

Cheek patch

20-6a. Stitching the fringe hair to the head
   b. Features

206 *Cyrus Centaur*

For a beard, cut a 1-inch strip of fringe, then stitch it to the fabric directly below the mouth.

Glue the orange felt cheek patches over the dots marked on the fabric below the eyes. When the glue has dried, stitch the patches to the fabric.

For the tail, cut 12 lengths of black rug yarn, each 18 inches. Thread a sharp, large-eyed needle with one length of yarn. Stitch the yarn through the fabric on the centaur's rump where a tail would originate. Half of the

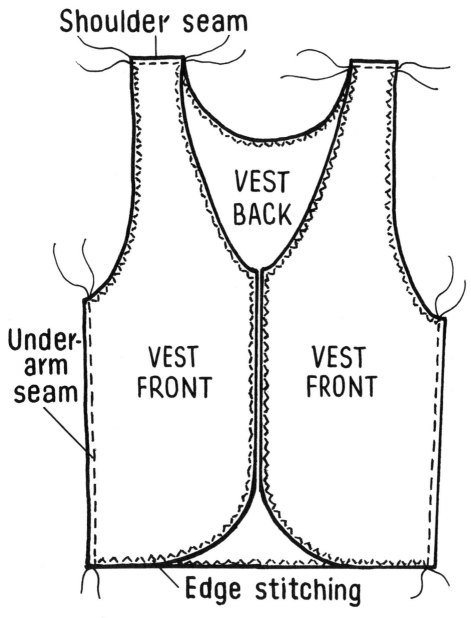

20-7   Stitching the front pieces of the vest to the back and edge stitching the raw edges

length of yarn should be on each side of the point where the needle penetrates the fabric. Remove the needle and tie the two ends of yarn in a secure knot (Fig. 9-5b). Stitch and tie the remaining pieces of yarn to the rump in the same manner, grouping the pieces as close together as possible. To make the tail thicker and curlier, unravel the yarn. Trim the ends of the tail if necessary.

STEP FIVE

Note: ¼-inch seams allowed.

Cyrus Centaur wears a furry vest that is very easy to make. Begin by stitching one front vest piece to the back vest piece at the shoulder seam and at the underarm seam (Fig. 20-7). Stitch the second front vest piece to the back vest piece at the shoulder seam and at the underarm seam. Trim the seams to ⅛ inch. To finish the vest, topstitch around each armhole edge, around the neck edge, around the base, and along the front edges of the vest. Use a narrow zigzag stitch and sew as close to the edge of the fabric as possible. If you do not have a zigzag stitch on your machine, you can finish the edges by hand with an overcast stitch to keep the raw edges from unraveling. The stitches should be spaced evenly apart and be of uniform depth for a neat, decorative finish.

Cyrus Centaur is ready to stamp his hoof and gallop into the affection of his new master.

Glossary

Appliqué: A separate piece of fabric that is glued and stitched to the main body of the toy or to another piece of fabric.

Armature: A wire frame placed inside a toy to give it structural support.

Base End: The end of an assembly, such as arms, legs, ears, etc., that is attached to the main body of the toy.

Baste: To stitch temporarily with a long loose stitch, either by hand or machine. The basting is usually removed after a more permanent stitching has been accomplished.

Bias Tape: A pre-cut and pre-folded strip of fabric used for binding raw edges when making clothing or used to make an applied casing for elastic.

Casing: A tunnel or hem of fabric stitched along one or both edges with the ends left open, used to hold elastic.

Easing: Stitching slowly and stretching or gathering the edge of a gusset to fit the curves of the piece to which it is being stitched.

Gathering: Drawing up fabric on a line of stitching, thereby creating soft folds.

Gusset: A strip of fabric that is stitched between two main pieces of a toy to make it more three-dimensional.

Hem: A finishing touch where the raw edge of a piece of fabric is turned up and stitched to the inside. The lower edge of a dress is usually hemmed.

Markings: Dots, dotted lines, notches, letters, and numbers which are transferred from the pattern to the fabric to aid in assembly of the toys.

Nap: A soft or fuzzy surface texture which some fabrics, such as corduroy, possess. A nap can be brushed smooth in one direction.

Outer Edge: The perimeter or boundary of a piece of fabric.

Pattern: A piece of paper cut to a particular shape that is pinned to fabric and used as a cutting guide.

Pile: A fabric woven with threads that stand up and give a soft, deep surface texture.

Raw Edge: The unfinished boundary or outer edge of a piece of fabric which has not been hemmed.

Right Side: The side of the fabric which will show when the toy or garment is completed.

Seam: A line of stitching that holds two or more pieces of fabric together.

Seam Line: The line along which the stitching that holds two or more pieces of fabric together is placed.

Skein: A length of yarn packaged in a loose coil.

Snap Closure: A metal fastener which can be sewn onto fabric to hold two edges together. They cannot take a lot of stress.

Stitch: To sew two or more pieces of fabric together with thread.

Stitching Line: Defined in this book as those markings transferred from the pattern to the fabric and then stitched to create joints or the illusion of fingers and toes.

Top Stitching: Stitching done on the right side of the fabric, sometimes parallel to a seam or an edge.

Turning to the Inside: Turning or folding fabric so that wrong side touches wrong side.

Turning to the Outside: Turning or folding fabric so that right side touches right side.

Wrong Side: The side of the fabric that isn't visible when the toy or garment is completed.

Zigzag: A special machine stitch. When stitches are set close together, it can be used to appliqué. When stitches are set at varying widths, it can be used as a decorative stitch.

Charlene Davis Roth

While Charlene grew up in North Syracuse, New York, and has spent much time on a family farm, her life has been a conglomerate of city and country for quite sometime.

Charlene studied art at the New York State University College at Plattsburg and at the Cooper Union School of Fine Arts in New York City. Then, she was working with an acetylene torch, designing large metal sculptures. Charlene now creates at her sewing machine.

Charlene's first encounter with toymaking was at age eight when her aunt fashioned a stuffed hippo and butterfly from a story Charlene had written and illustrated.

Since her renewed interest, Charlene's toymaking has become a full-time job. The Roths' three-year-old daughter, Amy, has been a major source of inspiration and one of Charlene's most avid fans. Mythology, fairy tales, children's stories, trips to the zoo, and visits to her family's farm have all inspired Charlene. The patterns, colors, and designs of the fabrics themselves often suggest ideas for the toys.

Together with her husband, Jerry, the Roths have written a successful book: *Toys: A Step-by-Step Guide to Creative Toymaking.* Jerry researched and wrote the narrative, while Charlene designed and sketched the wooden, cloth, and papier-mâché toys.

In addition to her creative and imaginative animal designs, Charlene has crafted all types of puppets, dolls, mobiles, and games. She has also proven to be a talented painter and author, contributing articles to *American Home Magazine, Creative Crafts Magazine,* and *Natural Living Magazine.* In 1968, she was invited to be a member of the New York State Craftsmen and has since received numerous awards and honorable mentions at craft fairs throughout New York State. Charlene's stuffed toys are favorites in many New York City boutiques.